Whitehall and the Commonwealth

LIBRARY OF POLITICAL STUDIES

GENERAL EDITOR:
PROFESSOR H. VICTOR WISEMAN

Department of Government
University of Exeter

Whitehall and the Commonwealth

British Departmental Organisation
for Commonwealth Relations, 1900-1966

by J. A. Cross
Lecturer in Politics
University College, Cardiff

LONDON

ROUTLEDGE AND KEGAN PAUL

NEW YORK: THE HUMANITIES PRESS

First published 1967
by Routledge and Kegan Paul Ltd
Broadway House, 68-74 Carter Lane
London, E.C.4.

Printed and Bound in Great Britain by
Bookprint Limited, London and Crawley

General editor's introduction

This series of paper-back monographs is designed primarily to meet the needs of students of government, politics, or political science in Universities and other institutions providing courses leading to degrees. Each volume aims to provide a brief general introduction indicating the significance of its topic, e.g. executives, parties, pressure groups, etc., and then a longer 'case study' relevant to the general topic. First year students will thus be introduced to the kind of detailed work on which all generalisations must be based, while more mature students will have an opportunity to become acquainted with recent original research in a variety of fields. The series will eventually provide a comprehensive coverage of most aspects of political science in a more interesting and fundamental manner than in the large volume which often fails to compensate by breadth what it inevitably lacks in depth.

This volume on Whitehall and the Commonwealth, while of great interest in itself, since Britain has for so long been the centre of an Empire and a Commonwealth, throws light also on the structure of central government departments and the administrative and political factors which influence the redistribution of functions between them. The internal working of departments and the role of the civil service are also illustrated. At a time when the last Colonial Secretary has hung his picture in the Colonial Office and nearly two hundred years of history have come to an end, this volume is both a record of the past and a document pointing to the future.

H. V. W.

Contents

   *Discussion of a C.R.O.-Colonial Office merger
   from 1954. Strongly advocated by 1960 Estimates
   Committee report. No immediate Government
   action to implement, but a single Secretary of State
   from 1962. Decision to merge announced February
   1964. New Labour Government initially delayed
   action (and re-appointed two Secretaries of State),
   but merger eventually took place 1st August, 1966.*

   *Britain unique in the Commonwealth in having
   separate Commonwealth relations department.
   Arguments for a merger with the Foreign Office
   advanced both during and after the war, but resisted
   by the Government and most informed opinion.
   The Plowden Report on overseas representational
   services published in February 1964: against a
   merger in present circumstances but thought it in
   'the logic of events'. A combined C.R.O.-Foreign
   Office Diplomatic Service set up; increasing
   operational liaison. The objections to a merger
   examined.*

   *Commonwealth conference functions used as
   argument for separate Commonwealth Office. The
   1964 Commonwealth Heads of Government
   Conference adopted – rather surprisingly – a
   proposal for a Commonwealth-based secretariat. A
   comparison with the reception of earlier secretariat
   proposals. The Secretariat set up, 1965. Its
   implications for the Commonwealth Office.*

I

Introduction

The aim of this study is to trace the evolution of British departmental organisation for Commonwealth relations during the twentieth century. It does not attempt to deal, other than incidentally, with the growth of the Empire-Commonwealth in this period or with the structure and organisation of the modern Commonwealth. There is, however, a close relationship between the two themes for Britain's Whitehall organisation in the Commonwealth field has had to keep in some sort of correspondence with the changing status of the constituent territories of the Empire-Commonwealth and the development of the Commonwealth association.

As convenient a symbol as any of the position the then self-governing communities (Canada, Australia, New Zealand, South Africa and Newfoundland) had reached by the beginning of the First World War – when they had achieved virtually complete control over their internal and trade affairs but when the 'diplomatic unity of the British Empire' under British leadership was still more or less intact – was the adoption, at the 1907 Colonial Conference, of the term 'Dominion' to differentiate them from the dependent crown colonies. By the end of the same year a Dominions Department was established inside the Colonial Office (then responsible for both self-governing and dependent colonies) to handle their affairs for the most part separately from the other work of the Office. In July 1925 the Dominions Department became formally separate from the Colonial Office as the Dominions Office, some 15 months before the Imperial Conference of 1926 defined (in the 'Balfour Report') the relationship of complete equality – in external, as well as internal affairs – between the Dominions and Britain. The separation was for some years, however, more apparent than real, for until 1947 the two Offices shared the same building and certain common services, had a joint establishment and, until 1930, the same minister. In 1947 came Indian independence and the consequent revolutionary change in the structure and nature of the Commonwealth. The independent, freely-associated part was now, in population, considerably greater than the part for which the Colonial Office was directly responsible, and it was no longer either predominantly European in race or, when India adopted a republican constitution (an example subsequently followed by many other member countries), all formally linked by 'common allegiance' to the Crown as were the 'Old Dominions'. It was thus symbolic that it was in 1947 that the Dominions Office should, under its new name of Commonwealth Relations Office, lose any remaining vestiges of inferiority to its Colonial Office parent and become a fully autonomous department. Ten years later the story of independent nationhood in the Commonwealth began its last and most crowded chapter with the granting of independence to the Gold Coast, which, as Ghana, became the first indigenous African member of the Commonwealth. Between 1957 and the middle of 1966, seventeen territories for which the Colonial Office had been responsible, with a total population of some ninety million, had achieved independence within the Commonwealth and, as a consequence, had their relations with Britain transferred from the Colonial Office, with its *administrative* responsibilities, to the Commonwealth Relations Office, with its *diplomatic* responsibilities. On 1st August, 1966, the departmental development came full circle when the Colonial Office ceased to exist as a separate department and became the Dependent Territories Division of the Commonwealth Relations Office, under its new designation of Commonwealth Office. But while there is some resemblance to the 1907 departmental pattern the circumstances have, of course, completely changed: unlike the 1907 Colonial Office the predominant section in the 1966 Commonwealth Office, reflecting the nature of the modern Commonwealth, is that dealing with the independent members of the Commonwealth.

Although the broad theme to which the study of departmental organisation for Commonwealth relations is most obviously relevant is that of the development of the Commonwealth as an association of independent nations, the study illustrates also a facet of British administrative practice. The existence of a department specifically to perform the function of supervising Britain's Commonwealth relationships may be seen as an example of the functional principle for allocating responsibilities between departments on which the Haldane Report of 1918 laid such stress. But the actual operation of the Office reveals that complexity of the workings of government which attempts to establish 'principles of organisation' tend to underestimate. Looked at in one way, Commonwealth relations may constitute a major function, but in another – as the more than twenty Commonwealth member countries are scattered over the globe – it is a regional or 'place' responsibility. And in yet another aspect of its role the Commonwealth Office, as the voice of the Commonwealth in the Whitehall policy-formulating process, is a 'clientele' department, acting as a kind of pressure group and focal point for the Commonwealth.

In its internal organisation, too, the Commonwealth relations department has had to evolve some compromise between the rival merits of arranging its business by area or subject. The latter criterion has become increasingly important and nowadays any important policy question involving a single Commonwealth country is the concern of several divisions of the Office; nevertheless there is still some organisation by area, cut across by the subject divisions.

It is unlikely that the Commonwealth Office of 1966 represents the culmination of the evolutionary process in Whitehall organisation for Commonwealth relations. As Commonwealth membership has expanded so has the association become more diversified and the links between members more tenuous – in many cases weaker than their links with more immediate non-Commonwealth neighbours. Has the 'Commonwealth relationship' become so attenuated that it no longer ranks a Whitehall department to itself? Is there still a Commonwealth relations 'function' distinct from a general external relations 'function'? It is now, indeed, widely argued that Commonwealth relations are merely an aspect of British overseas policy as a whole and the appropriate department for their oversight is the Foreign Office, with which the Commonwealth Office should be merged. Steps have recently been taken to combine the staffs of the two departments into a unified Diplomatic Service, but they remain departmentally distinct. A full merger is clearly in 'the logic of events' but it is worth noting that administrative logic has by no means been the only – or even the most important – determinant of departmental responsibilities in Whitehall.

II

The Colonial Office and the Self-Governing Colonies before 1907

At the beginning of the twentieth century the organisation in Whitehall for the supervision of Britain's vast imperial responsibilities was almost as heterogeneous as the empire itself. There was the India Office, established in 1858 immediately after the Mutiny, which looked after the great Indian Empire in virtual isolation from the rest of Britain's imperial possessions, and whose only general imperial concern seemed to be the condition of Indians living in other parts of the Empire. Actual administration in India was in the hands of the quasi-autonomous Government of India under the Viceroy, an office considered by many to be the greatest in the Queen's service. The Foreign Office, too, had direct imperial administrative responsibilities, retaining the Sudan until its independence in 1955 and controlling the other products of British participation in the 'scramble for Africa' – in west, east and central Africa – until they were transferred to the Colonial Office between 1900 and 1905. But its main interest in the empire was, of course, as it affected Britain's relations with foreign powers.

The chief, if not the exclusive, imperial department was the Colonial Office, responsible for the administration of various kinds of colonies in Europe, North America, the West Indies, Australasia, the Pacific, south-east Asia and

Africa. In each colony the head of administration was the governor (or governor-general in the larger self-governing colonies), as agent of the British Government in general and the Colonial Office in particular. The chief distinguishing feature between colonies in practice was the degree to which the governor exercised direct discretionary control. In the crown colonies and protectorates his power was absolute, and here the Colonial Office exercised a detailed administrative oversight of the actions of the governor and the affairs of the colony. But from the middle of the nineteenth century the settlement colonies in North America, Australasia and southern Africa were progressively securing autonomy in their domestic and commercial affairs, with a consequent diminution in the influence of the governor and the Colonial Office. On domestic matters the convention was firmly established that the governors of 'responsible' or self-governing colonies acted on the advice of their elected ministers, and only on 'imperial' matters – affecting the empire as a whole – were they expected to refer questions to the Colonial Office. But colonial governments began to trench on this field too, a process in which Canada led the way, as in so many other aspects of the development of the Empire-Commonwealth. Canada had vindicated its fiscal autonomy as long ago as 1859, following a successful brush with the British authorities over the proposed Canadian imposition of a protective tariff. This led on naturally to the negotiation of commercial treaties with foreign powers, culminating in 1907 in the conclusion of a Canadian trade agreement with France after negotiations conducted entirely by Canadian representatives, the British ambassador to France merely adding his signature to the final document.

By 1907 the self-governing colonies, or 'Dominions' as they were called from that year – Canada, Australia, New Zealand, the South African colonies (two of which had just regained responsible government after the temporary

6

setback of the South African War) and, to a lesser extent, Newfoundland – had, in fact if not in form, control over their internal affairs and their trade with other countries. Britain's powers remained complete in law but were clearly obsolescent in convention, and it was rare indeed for the Colonial Office to win (or, indeed, try to win) a constitutional argument against the wishes of the Dominion concerned. In most legislative fields the Dominions were in practice autonomous, and it was in very few that the British Parliament continued to legislate intra-imperially – merchant shipping, copyright, naturalisation, and the control of armed forces abroad being among them. But even on these subjects it legislated only after a consensus had been obtained and in the interests of convenient uniformity between a closely-associated group of countries, on behalf of the group as a whole. The parliamentary supremacy of Westminster was a symbolic, rather than practical, irritant to Dominion national pride.

The United Kingdom continued to control foreign political relations on behalf of the empire. But here again the restriction on Dominion autonomy was not noticeably onerous. The Dominions were concerned with their own immediate, concrete interests, and these did not at that time extend to the wider issues with which British foreign policy had to deal, and for which Britain alone had the necessary technical resources (including the Foreign Office and its diplomatic service). Dominion interest in foreign affairs was, for the most part, local and particular: it was with such issues as Alaska, the New Hebrides, Samoa and the negotiation of commercial agreements directly affecting their trade that the Dominions were individually concerned, rather than with the complex ramifications of the European balance of power. But as this was a period of acute imperial rivalries between European powers the exposed position of some of the Dominions – particularly the proximity of Australia and New Zealand to the Pacific, where British, French and

German interests were often in conflict – meant that the Colonial Office (or, rather, the Foreign Office through its mediation) had to exert some care to see that ebullient colonial nationalists did not jeopardise Britain's relations with other great powers. At various times governments in Newfoundland (in fishery disputes with France and the United States), Australia and New Zealand (constantly pressing for the extension of British influence in the Pacific) were the cause of acute embarrassment to the Colonial Office and the British Government as a whole. The real power which the British Government exerted here – unlike that it exerted over Dominion internal affairs or, to a lesser degree, their trade relations – was that the active co-operation of Britain was essential for the realisation of Dominion aims.

The Colonial Office was not, of course, the only Whitehall department whose responsibilities impinged on the Dominions. The Foreign Office, the Board of Trade, the Admiralty, the War Office, the Post Office – all these and several more were concerned departmentally with relations with the Dominions. But the formal channel of communication between the British Government or Government departments and the Dominions lay through the Colonial Office, whose principal role in this field was as the co-ordinating department in Whitehall for matters affecting the Dominions. If, for example, a Dominion government wished to contact officially any British Government department it had to send a dispatch or minute through the governor-general or governor to the Colonial Office, which would then forward a copy of it to the department or departments concerned, adding any comments it thought appropriate. In probably the great majority of cases this was purely a 'post office' function, but the Colonial Office viewed its own role as much more positive than this: it was to ensure the consistent application of imperial policy in every field concerning the empire. This involved making its fellow-departments aware of any general imperial needs which might cut across ordinary departmental policy, and 'vetting' departmental replies before dispatch in case they were incompatible with general imperial policy or, sometimes even more important, likely to offend Dominion susceptibilities unnecessarily. The Colonial Office thus conceived of itself as an expert assessor of imperial needs rather than simply as a medium of communication.

The internal organisation of the Colonial Office to deal with its wide-ranging responsibilities was based primarily on the geographical principle. Thus early in the twentieth century there was a West Indian department, an Eastern department, two West African departments, two South African departments (a sign of the extra work the South African War imposed on the Office), and a North American and Australian department. Apart from legal work, and the establishments, patronage and related work of the General department and the Chief Clerk, each geographical department had to deal with everything that concerned its colonies, a factor which, according to the description of the Office in 1909 by a future Permanent Under-Secretary, 'sometimes tended to create a sense of possession and rivalry' (Parkinson, 36).

Although the Colonial Office was organised by geography rather than by status, the Office had long been aware of the distinction between self-governing colony work and that for crown colonies. Britain's relations with her self-governing colonies was 'political rather than colonial', a former Colonial Secretary, Lord Carnarvon, had observed as long ago as 1870 (Farr, 309), while an Office memorandum of 1888 recorded that 'the concession of self-government to many of the great colonies has relieved the Colonial Office of one class of business only to be succeeded by another of a still more anxious character, particularly as regards foreign relations and international arrangements' (C. 5545, 458). Some limited administrative recognition of the special position of the self-governing colonies within the Office had been given in 1867, when the Eastern department lost all its Australian and New Zealand business to the North American department which, under the name of North American and Australian department, supervised the affairs of the main self-governing colonies until 1907 (Pugh, 1964, 9–10). Only the South African colonies remained outside its orbit, although the North American and Australian and South African departments worked together to service the periodic Colonial Conferences.

The conference system itself was the one enduring result of the intense, if somewhat academic, discussion of the future organisational structure of the empire, which was a feature of the latter years of the nineteenth and the early years of the twentieth century. The foundation of the Imperial Federation League in 1884 served to canalise the various federal proposals which were being adumbrated, while such factors as the assumption of the Colonial Secretaryship by Joseph Chamberlain in 1895, the active colonial support for Britain in the South African War, and the debate on tariff reform for imperial purposes seemed to produce an atmosphere uniquely favourable to institutional reform of the empire. The first Colonial Conference had been held in London in 1887, and subsequent meetings took place in 1897, 1902 and 1907 (there was also a subsidiary conference in Canada in 1894). The conferences – especially those held in 1897 and 1902, during Chamberlain's tenure of office – were in form an occasional advisory council to the responsible British minister, the Colonial Secretary, and composed of the premiers of the self-governing colonies. But they became more than this, a conference of governments, as the assembly was described at the last Colonial Conference in 1907.

The point on which imperial reformers seized was the question of maintaining continuity in the rather lengthy intervals between conferences. This, it was argued, necessitated a secretariat or permanent commission based in London on which the Dominions should be represented, perhaps by their high commissioners or agents-general in London. It would be an imperial rather than a British (or rather, Colonial Office) body, and would provide material for conference members which had been sifted by the Dominion governments as well as by the British Government. Such a secretariat formed an integral part of the scheme for an imperial 'council of advice' worked out between 1903 and 1907 by a distinguished private committee presided over by Sir Frederick Pollock; and it seemed to have been given some official sanction when it appeared as a proposal in a dispatch which Alfred Lyttelton, Chamberlain's successor as Colonial Secretary, sent to the self-governing colonies in April 1905 (Cd. 2785). This suggested the replacement of the Colonial Conference by an Imperial Council (including, when appropriate, India and the crown colonies as well as the self-governing colonies) and the setting up of an advisory joint permanent commission. The latter body, comprising representatives of the United Kingdom and the colonies, would keep records and act as a secretariat, suggest policy on questions referred to it, and prepare questions for the consideration of the Council.

Although they were not in themselves federal, such schemes, if implemented, could be seen by ardent advocates of imperial federation as a modest but significant step in the direction of a centralised political organisation for the empire as a whole. The insuperable obstacle to this final consummation – and indeed to many less ambitious plans – was the Dominion emphasis, not on the imperial whole, but on their separate national identities – a fact of which the Liberal Government in Britain from the end of 1905 was perhaps necessarily more aware than its Conservative predecessor. The later champions of imperial federation, notably Lionel Curtis, who was a leading member of the Round Table movement founded in 1909, were at pains to point out that it would not in fact arrest the growth of national autonomy nor limit equality of status, but rather complete that development by giving the Dominions a share in deciding the issues of peace and war which touched them so nearly.

The attitude of the Dominions to plans for imperial reorganisation were not, however, always wholly negative. Canada, it was true, was primarily concerned to secure *de facto* autonomy and had no imperial aims beyond that, once the peaceful intentions of its great southern neighbour, the United States, had become established. There was too much to be done to open up their vast country to make Canadians wish to get involved with imperial policy-making and, as they saw it, the maelstrom of European politics. Canada wanted to be left alone to develop its resources rather than form part of a great imperial organisation. But, on the other side of the world, Australia and New Zealand, while also concerned to vindicate their national identities, wished to have a voice in that imperial policy which Britain monopolised to itself. They felt acutely their isolated position in face of European colonial rivalries in the Pacific and the rapid growth of Japanese power, and realised their vital need for British protection. Hence their demand was for consultation with the British Government when their interests were involved.

The contrast between the Canadian and Australian attitudes was personified in Sir Wilfrid Laurier, Prime Minister of Canada from 1896 to 1911, and Alfred Deakin, a leading political figure in Victoria before the formation of the Commonwealth of Australia in 1900 and thereafter Australian Prime Minister for most of the period between 1903 and 1910. Laurier wished to develop Canadian nationalism with the minimum commitment to wider imperial purposes and was thus inevitably the defender of the imperial *status quo* for fear that change would bring added involvement; while Deakin stressed the role that the Dominions must play in shaping those wider imperial purposes. Laurier, now that Canadian autonomy had been gained in practice, was quite content with the way the Colonial Office discharged its responsibilities in respect of the self-governing communities. Deakin, on the other hand, considered the Colonial Office inimical to his ideal of real imperial consultation and active imperial policies, and wished the affairs of the Dominions to be removed altogether from its sphere; he looked to an independent conference secretariat to achieve this. Laurier's attitude to the empire was passive, Deakin's activist. The Colonial Office was quite aware of the contrast: 'When we please Deakin, we offend Laurier', Hopwood, the Permanent Under-Secretary wrote in 1908 (C.O. 532/7, No. 38604). The Office knew it could rely on Laurier to resist any organisational changes which it itself found distasteful.

Schemes for imperial reorganisation were an implicit criticism of the way in which the Colonial Office conducted the affairs of the self-governing colonies. Deakin, more than anyone else, brought these criticisms into the open. As far back as the Colonial Conference of 1887 he had castigated the 'natural *vis inertiæ* of the Office and twenty years later, at the last Colonial Conference, he delivered a full-scale attack (Fiddes, 245). He complained particularly of the 'attitude of mind' of the officials: 'A certain impenetrability; a certain remoteness, perhaps geographically justified; a certain weariness of people much depressed with affairs, and greatly over-burdened, whose natural desire is to say "Kindly postpone this; do not press that, do not trouble us; what does it matter? We have enough to do already: you are a self-governing community, why not manage to carry on without worrying us?" '

The main reason for this attitude, Deakin felt, was that the whole Office was imbued, both consciously and unconsciously, with 'principles of government properly applicable to crown colonies' which 'are very foreign, and in some cases almost antagonistic, to the principles on which the affairs of the self-governing colonies are conducted'. The only remedy was the complete separation of the affairs of the self-governing colonies from the other work of the Colonial Office and the institution of a conference secretariat responsible, not to the Colonial Office, but to the conference itself, through the British Prime Minister.

The Colonial Office was conscious of such criticisms and some of its officials were prepared to concede that some changes might be necessary. Frederick Graham, the Senior Assistant Under-Secretary, in a memorandum which he prepared in December 1904 (C.O. 323/511, No. 10975), outlined a rather impracticable scheme involving a re-organised Colonial Office which would deal with matters 'peculiar to some particular Colony' (e.g., constitutional questions, public works, education, treatment of aborigines, finance and inland revenue) and the creation of 'a new Imperial Department concerned with matters common to several or all parts of the Empire' (e.g., defence, tariffs, navigation and external trade, immigration, copyright). Curiously, Graham rejected both the separation of self-governing colony work from crown colony work and any attempt at geographical sub-division as being administratively inconsistent: his own division was on the basis neither of status nor of geography, but of subject matter. There was, however, a possible foreshadowing of the change made three years later in the marginal comment by Sir Montagu Ommanney, the Permanent Under-Secretary, on Graham's assertion that it was not easy to see how the Office could be divided without a sacrifice of administrative consistency: 'Is there', Ommanney asked, 'a shadow of administrative consistency between the self-governing and Crown Colonies?'

The approach of the 1907 Colonial Conference, at which the formidable Deakin would represent Australia, impelled further Office consideration of organisational change. The idea of a conference secretariat outside Colonial Office control was rejected by all the senior officials, one of them remarking that it was 'rather hard on this office that we should be superseded, or our work greatly hampered' by such an institution (C.O. 323/503, No. 11053). They had been against the ideas in the 1905 Lyttelton dispatch (C.O. 323/511, No. 10975), and the new Liberal Colonial Secretary, Lord Elgin, had no disposition to take his predecessor's initiative any further. However, both Elgin and Sir Francis Hopwood, Ommanney's successor as Permanent Under-Secretary, prepared plans for a permanent conference secretariat *within* the Colonial Office. In addition, the prospect in 1906–7 of two more colonies – the Transvaal and Orange River Colony – joining (or rather re-joining) the ranks of those enjoying responsible government seemed to make some reorganisation of the Office desirable on administrative grounds. But probably the major reason for the Colonial Secretary's proposals at the 1907 conference was, as Elgin later admitted to his successor, Lord Crewe, to provide 'a countercheck to the . . . dangerous movement for the establishment of an authority outside the control of the Minister who is responsible for Colonial Affairs' (Kendle thesis, 172).

At the conference itself, despite the vehemence of Deakin's criticisms, supported in part by Jameson, the premier of Cape Colony, Elgin was able to avoid any commitment to fundamental change. He was aided by Laurier, who expressed himself as quite satisfied with existing departmental arrangements and was rootedly opposed to Deakin's scheme for a conference secretariat, on grounds both of lack of clear ministerial responsibility and of potential danger to Dominion autonomy. Nevertheless Elgin did give a pledge, though in very general terms, to constitute a department dealing exclusively with the self-governing colonies or Dominions (as it was decided at the conference they might informally be called), with which would be connected a permanent conference secretariat. The only small satisfaction imperial reformers gained was the resolution to regularise the conference system, under the title 'Imperial Conference', on a quadrennial basis, with provision for subsidiary conferences on particular topics.

III

The 1907 Reorganisation and its Aftermath

It may well have been that some of the prime ministers and others in the Dominions interpreted Elgin's somewhat imprecise pledge as the institution of a new department to deal with their affairs outside the Colonial Office. But this was certainly not the intention of either Elgin or his officials. A Colonial Office letter to the Treasury in August 1907 (C.O. 323/534, No. 29255A), outlining the proposed reorganisation, stated quite clearly that the Secretary of State did not regard the creation of a separate department as either justifiable or necessary 'in the present circumstances' as it would involve considerable duplication of work. He was, moreover, 'anxious, on financial as well as on other grounds, to retain the Imperial Secretariat as an integral part of the establishment of the Colonial Office'. He thought that the reorganisation planned would 'be able to satisfy the pledge given by His Majesty's Government without making any further call upon the public purse' (an argument clearly calculated to please the Treasury).

The Colonial Office as reorganised (from 1st December, 1907) was divided into three departments or divisions (the terms were used interchangeably, although 'department' was the more frequent appellation): Dominions, Crown Colonies, and Legal and General – providing, it was claimed, for 'the easier and more symmetrical working of the office'. The Crown Colonies Department dealt with West Indian, Eastern, West and East African colonies, Gibraltar, Malta and Cyprus. The Legal and General Department (soon contracted to the old title of General Department) represented a merger of the legal work of the Office with that performed by the Chief Clerk and the former General department, including audit, patronage, defence schemes and establishment questions, and thus overlapped with the work of the other two departments. From 1911 it ceased to have the same status as the others and became, in effect, part of the Crown Colonies Department: the administrative dichotomy between Dominion and colony work thus became clearer.

The Dominions Department took over the work of the North American and Australian and South African departments apart from all their crown colony work other than that connected with colonies 'whose interests are so closely related to those of adjoining self-governing Colonies that the conduct of their business at this office must necessarily be entrusted to the same hands' (Cd. 3795, 4). Its territorial responsibilities thus included – in addition to Canada, Australia, the Australian States, New Zealand, Newfoundland, and the four colonies which three years later joined in the Union of South Africa (Cape Colony, Natal, Transvaal and Orange River Colony) – Fiji, the Western Pacific colonies, Basutoland, Bechuanaland, Swaziland and Rhodesia. The departmental officials, as in the pre-1907 Colonial Office, still worked in two recognisable sections – one concerned with South Africa, the other with North America and Australasia. The department also dealt with emigration questions, supervising the work of the Emigrants' Information Office, and was represented on the Advisory Committee on Commercial Intelligence of the Board of Trade.

The actual relationship of the Imperial Conference Secretariat to the Dominions Department was left – at any rate publicly – somewhat vague, as if the Colonial

Office were reluctant to admit to the Dominions that it was in fact fully integrated with the department. Elgin's dispatch to the Dominions explaining the reorganisation, which was circulated in September 1907 (Cd. 3795), described the secretariat as being 'linked' to the Dominions Department 'without being entirely merged into it' and went on: 'The Secretary will be a member of the department but he will also have, as occasion requires, direct access to the Secretary of State.' It is understandable that there should have been some confusion in the Dominions as to its position (for example, in one of New Zealand's resolutions for the 1911 conference, proposing that the staff of the secretariat should be integrated with the Dominions Department) – and indeed senior officials in the department themselves held differing views about the functions, if not the status, of the secretariat. Sir Charles Lucas, the head of the Dominions Department, wanted an active secretariat which would initiate discussion and action, while most of his colleagues (including Hartmann Just, the Secretary of the Imperial Conference) favoured inactivity for fear of offending against Dominion autonomy.

In practice the secretariat was an integral part of the Dominions Department, and its members had ordinary departmental duties as well as their conference responsibilities. In 1910 Just was able to record, with obvious satisfaction, that whereas Deakin may have conceived of a conference secretariat which would 'swallow up the Dominions department . . . the reverse process is that which is actually taking place' (C.O. 532/35, No. 25309). And when, in the following year, Just succeeded Lucas as head of the department, the two posts of Secretary of the Imperial Conference and departmental head were combined: the 'swallowing up' process was complete.

For the staff of the Dominions Department it seemed to be of more than academic interest that the department should 'swallow-up' the secretariat rather than 'the reverse process': a really independent conference secretariat, responsible as Deakin wished, to the conference members as a whole, might conceivably have assumed some of the functions of the Colonial Office and become an increasingly important channel of contact between the Dominions and Britain and with each other. But these fears may well have been exaggerated. It is difficult to discern at this time what were the 'inter-imperial' questions with which an independent secretariat would have been expected to deal. Under no circumstances would the British Government have consented to share its primary responsibility for defence and foreign policy, even if the Dominions had really wished it to do so, and thus these issues would presumably have been excluded from the secretariat's field of action. The treatment of Indians within the empire was another inter-imperial topic, but there is no reason to believe that an independent secretariat would have altered the existing situation or modified the acknowledged right of each Dominion to determine its own immigration policy. The major issues affecting the relations between Britain and the Dominions were in large part those which concerned one Dominion only or on which a Dominion desired to secure British help in order to advance its own interests, whether trade or strategic – and these were necessarily not inter-imperial in the true sense.

For the chief critics of the Colonial Office the 1907 reorganisation did not go nearly far enough. Deakin dismissed it as merely the renaming of a sub-department – although it could be taken as a small sign of grace that two years later he apparently did not wish to abolish the Dominions Department (C.O. 532/16, No. 35842). The man who, eighteen years later, as Colonial Secretary, presided over the separation of the Dominions Office from the Colonial Office, was touring Kenya and Uganda at the time the 1907 reorganisation took effect. It was these visits which convinced L. S. Amery that the separation of colonial from Dominion problems was no less necessary in the interests of the colonies than of the Dominions, since the 'combination of the two utterly different problems and relationships in a single office meant a laisser-faire outlook towards creative work in the Colonies . . . while it still retained an attitude of superiority and lack of understanding of democratic communities in dealing with the Dominions' (Amery, 1953, ii, 321).

Others were more optimistic, looking upon the Dominions Department as a step in the right direction. Lord Grey, Governor-General of Canada and an ardent imperialist, 'rejoiced' in the division of the Office and hoped that 'at no distant time' the Dominions Department would be handed over 'to an Imperial Minister under a roof of its own'. Hopwood, the Permanent Under-Secretary at the Colonial Office, thought Grey's views 'far too sanguine' but found them interesting because they revealed to the Office the Canadian interest in a matter which to Hopwood seemed 'comparatively unimportant' (Kendle thesis, 180–1).

But Grey's optimism rested upon knowledge of a surprising admission to him by Laurier, soon after the latter's return from the 1907 conference, that it might be wise to create 'a new and separate department' under a responsible minister to deal with the affairs of the Dominions. He had apparently been considering the idea during the conference but had had 'no time nor opportunity' to explore it. Two years later Grey informed Lord Crewe, Elgin's successor as Colonial Secretary, that Laurier might consider recommending for discussion at the forthcoming Imperial Conference (due in 1911) 'a separate Department with a roof and Minister of its own'. Crewe was understandably surprised at this change in Laurier's attitude, and although attracted by the idea of a separate ministry, he wondered whether Laurier's new views were prompted by dissatisfaction with the Colonial Office or a reconsideration of the whole question of Dominion-United Kingdom relations. He would want to be certain, Crewe told Grey, that such a step – quite apart from the expense or multi-plication of offices – would not be premature in the existing situation of the empire. Grey was able to assure Crewe that Laurier had no complaint against the Colonial Office but had simply examined the whole problem of imperial organisation. He (Laurier) was still hostile to any form of imperial secretariat – other than the existing one under Colonial Office control – and he would insist that the proposed separate department could only be discussed on the understanding that it would not involve the slightest risk to Dominion autonomy.

Crewe gradually became convinced that the change would have its advantages. In March 1910 he forecast in a public speech that the existing departmental arrangements by which the same minister was responsible for the business connected with 'the great Dominions' as well as 'all the rest of the Empire except India' was not likely to last permanently. The time might come 'at no very distant date' when matters relating to the Dominions might be entrusted to one minister and the affairs of crown colonies and protectorates, which was 'work of a very different kind', to another. Crewe confessed that he personally would regret such a change – not, however for any administrative reason but because he found 'the work connected with both equally interesting' (*The Times*, 16th March, 1910).

Soon after this, however, Laurier – under continuous pressure from his Governor-General, Grey, who was an enthusiastic advocate of the proposal – at last brought the question of a separate department before his Cabinet. Here he encountered unexpected opposition from one of its senior members, W. S. Fielding, the Minister of Finance, who was quite satisfied with existing British departmental arrangements. The Governor-General tried, unsuccessfully, to change Fielding's opinion in a series of private conversations. As a result Laurier refused to submit a conference resolution on the subject since the action did not have unanimous Cabinet support (Kendle thesis, 213–6). Thus this brief, and uncharacteristic, foray by Laurier into the reform of imperial organisation came – permanently – to an end (he was once again the defender of the *status quo* at the 1911 conference). It seems likely that it was more the advocacy of Grey than Laurier's own predilections which kept the project going at all.

But others were propagating reorganisation schemes, in particular the newly-formed Round Table movement, with Lionel Curtis and L. S. Amery among its members. Curtis, after visits to Canada and South Africa, left for Australia in June 1910 and while there made certain proposals to the New Zealand Government through Lord Islington, the Governor, and these formed the basis of several of the long list of resolutions submitted by New Zealand for the Imperial Conference (Kendle, 1965, 105, 108–10). Amery, too, was active. In a leader in *The Times* in February 1908 he had suggested two permanent under-secretaries at the Colonial Office – one for the Dominions and one for the crown colonies – and in an address to the Royal Colonial Institute in June 1910 he returned to the theme of departmental reorganisation (Amery, 1912, 282–3). To get rid of 'the last vestige of the old colonial relationship of subordination to a British administrative department' it was necessary, Amery argued, to separate 'the office of Minister for Imperial Affairs' from the administration of crown colonies. The right person to deal with inter-imperial relations was either the Prime Minister himself or a deputy, who might conveniently combine the office of Secretary for Imperial Affairs with that of Lord President of the Council. Amery looked upon this as 'completing that division between the work of administering the crown colonies and of corresponding with the Dominions on which Mr. Deakin laid such stress in 1907'. A Dominions Department had been set up inside the Colonial Office as a result of Deakin's 'spirited protest', but 'it would be an enormous step forward towards Imperial union if the

c

Dominions once knew that the transaction of their affairs had been taken out of the Colonial Office altogether and entrusted to a real Imperial Office with a new tradition and an outlook corresponding to the altered constitutional relation . . .' The new office would also be the appropriate home for the secretariat of the Imperial Conference. The 'compromise accepted in 1907 of a secretariat directly under the Colonial Office, and without initiative' had resulted in 'practically nothing being done'. The fact that its members were also engaged on other onerous duties in the Office was a 'clear indication of its relative unimportance from the official point of view'.

Just a fortnight after Amery's Royal Colonial Institute address, the subject of Colonial Office reorganisation was brought up in the course of a Commons debate on the Colonial Office Estimates for 1910–11 (18 H.C.Deb., 956–1070). Several Conservatives urged the need for separating Dominions from crown colonies departmentally, one (Tryon), for instance, putting forward the much-repeated view that 'The mental attitude to be adopted towards our great self-governing Dominions . . . [is] . . . entirely different from that to be adopted to the crown colonies'; while another (Halford Mackinder) stressed the need for the Dominions Department and the conference secretariat to be concerned with inter-imperial relations, rather than with specific matters concerning one Dominion only. Seely, the Colonial Under-Secretary, was not encouraging, for he thought that the Dominions would be satisfied with nothing less than their affairs being in the hands of the British Prime Minister and 'If he does not find the time to do the work will not the Dominions be in a worse position than they are at the present moment?' The debate did not escape notice in the Dominions, however, and J. C. Smuts in South Africa was glad to detect in it 'a distinct movement in favour of the separation of the Dominions Department from the other branches of colonial administration'. He regarded the proposed change 'as a sign of the times and a step in the direction of the establishment of immediate relations between the Crown [rather than a British Government department] and the Dominion Governments' which he envisaged as the 'principal link between the constituent portions of the Empire' (Gladstone Papers, Add. MSS. 46004).

Despite Seely's somewhat negative attitude the Government was in fact so convinced that departmental arrangements for imperial affairs needed re-examination that a Cabinet committee on the subject, under Crewe's chairmanship, had been appointed a few days before the Commons' debate. In December 1910 Amery submitted to this committee a memorandum on similar lines to his Royal Colonial Institute address (Kendle, 1965, 104), but among the earliest material the committee considered were papers, both dated July 1910, by the two chief officials of the Dominions Department, Sir Charles Lucas, the head of the department, and Hartmann Just, the Secretary to the Imperial Conference (C.O. 886/4, Nos. 25 & 29).

Just was against any departmental change and maintained this attitude in all the subsequent discussions. The division of the Office, he wrote, would not be contemplated unless it were supposed to meet the wishes of the Dominions, since the present arrangement was perfectly adequate from the point of view of the British Government. But did the Dominions really desire a change? They appeared to want the Prime Minister to assume responsibility for their affairs, but this was impossible because he was too busy to perform the official and social duties which would be thrown upon him. Thus any arrangement by which the Prime Minister became the titular head of the department dealing with the Dominions would compel the devolution of the actual duties upon some other minister. This might lead, Just wrote in a passage which strikingly revealed the Colonial Office attitude to the Dominions, 'to a separate smaller office and the separate subordinate Ministers [i.e., subordinate to the Prime Minister] wishing to justify their separate existence by exceptional and increased activity . . . [with] . . . the danger that there would be greater interference with the self-governing Dominions and efforts to lead and urge forward. *So far the success of the administration of the self-governing Dominions has been due to the Colonial Office adopting the policy of non-interference and not forcing the pace.'* The advantage of retaining the present system was that the Dominions would continue to come within the responsibility of a prominent minister 'not exclusively occupied with their affairs and *therefore not likely to meddle unduly*; and the members of the Department would still work more in the shade than would be possible with a separate office' (Author's italics).

Lucas – who had already in Office discussions clashed with his colleague over the role of the secretariat, which he had wanted to bring out of 'the shade' – would have none of Just's devotion to the maintenance of the departmental *status quo*. He believed, he wrote in his Cabinet paper, that 'sooner or later' the Dominions Department must be taken out of the Colonial Office. The present position was 'a half-way compromise' and regarded as such. Having gone so far, the logical outcome was to go further: 'Having admitted that the work of the self-governing Dominions and that of the Crown Colonies should be kept strictly apart, it must probably be only a question of time to put them under separate roofs and separate Ministers.' Lucas did not think that the arguments against – including the possible expense and duplication of work, and the necessity for some colonial work (for example, the Pacific Islands and the High Commission Territories in South Africa) to go with the Dominions with which it was geographically related – outweighed those in favour of a change. And among the latter Lucas principally stressed that 'The future lies in recognising the growing equality of the self-governing Dominions with the mother country and eliminating the semblance of subordination. The proposed change would be a step in this direction.'

Lucas felt that the most appropriate minister to supervise the separate Dominions Department, in view of the Prime Minister's inability to assume the burden, would be the Lord President (echoing Amery's suggestion of the previous month). The Lord President, like the Prime Minister, had no specific departmental responsibilities, and as such would satisfy the Dominion desire to deal with the British Government as a whole rather than with a single departmental minister. But since he would necessarily be a member of the House of Lords (as all Lord Presidents were until the appointment of A. J. Balfour in 1919), the Prime Minister could perhaps act as the 'spokesman of the Dominions' in the Commons.

In October 1910 the conference resolutions put forward by the Dominions began arriving in the Colonial Office, and this intensified consideration of possible reorganisation. In the ensuing official minutes Just's influence was considerably more powerful than that of Lucas, who seems to have played very little part in them after submitting his Cabinet paper.

Among the twenty-one resolutions submitted by New Zealand (which included the suggestion of an apparently quasi-federal 'Imperial Council of State'), the one which directly raised the question of the internal organisation of the Office was that which proposed that the two sides of the Office should be separated at permanent under-secretary level (as Amery had suggested in 1908), while presumably retaining a single minister, to be renamed 'the Secretary of State for Imperial Affairs'. In addition, South Africa proposed that the work relating to the Dominions, including the secretariat, should be transferred to the Prime Minister. Other New Zealand resolutions were aimed at enhancing the role of the high commissioner as a channel of information and advice, while the Imperial

Council of State idea, if accepted, would obviously impinge on the work of the Dominions Department.

There were two main strands in the subsequent discussions: possible internal reorganisation of the Colonial Office, with which was essentially linked proposals for a change of responsible minister, or his designation, or both; and an extension of the consultative machinery of the Imperial Conference. Most of the issues raised in the discussion were conveniently reviewed in Cabinet papers prepared by the two Colonial Office ministers – by Seely, the Under-Secretary, in March 1911, and by his chief, Harcourt (who had succeeded Crewe as Colonial Secretary in November 1910) in the following month (C.O. 532/35, No. 25309). Seely's is of particular interest because though it does not seem to have influenced directly the proposals actually made by the Colonial Secretary at the conference in May 1911, it examines in some detail the organisational consequences of setting up a separate Dominions Office – fourteen years before the step was finally taken. And the arguments Seely deployed showed a significant development from his rather inflexible stance in the Commons' debate of the previous June.

There was no danger, Seely thought, of the minister in charge of a Dominions Office being 'inadequately occupied'. Although the papers dealt with by the Dominions Department were only about a quarter of all those dealt with by the Office as a whole, they frequently involved important and difficult questions of policy and probably constituted not far short of half those which had to be considered by the Secretary of State personally. In addition, a considerable proportion of the Colonial Secretary's time was devoted to receiving high commissioners and Dominion visitors and he had a very large personal correspondence with governors-general and governors.

Seely next dealt with the division of territorial responsibilities. It could be taken for granted, he thought, 'that the work of the South African Protectorates [the High

Commission Territories] must always be dealt with by the same officials who deal with matters relating to the Union of South Africa, with which the Protectorates are so closely connected'. A similar question arose in connection with Fiji and the Western Pacific; on the whole the balance of advantage, Seely considered, lay with the retention of this work by those who dealt with the Dominions.

The question of the staffing of the new office depended on whether the secretariat was to remain closely connected with the Dominions Department or to form a separate unit responsible only to the ministerial chiefs of the office. The former plan seemed to Seely to be better in every way and would conform to a vital principle of good administration – that there should be one permanent head of the whole office, responsible to the minister. On the assumption that the secretariat would be part of the office, the establishment of a separate Dominions Office would represent an increase of a Secretary of State, a Parliamentary and a Permanent Under-Secretary, a legal adviser, and two or three other administrative officials over the existing staff of the Dominions Department. Of the work at present done for the Dominions Department by the General Department, Seely envisaged that ceremonial and honours work (and presumably, although he did not refer to this, establishment work as well) would have to be transferred, while the new office would also need its own accounts and copying branches; it could share with the Colonial Office the services of the library and the printing department.

On the general question it seemed to Seely that there was no middle course between setting up a separate office and leaving the Colonial Office as it was, practically unchanged. As much separation had been effected within the Office as it was possible to achieve. He thought that the appointment of two permanent under-secretaries, one for Dominion and the other for crown colony work (as proposed by New Zealand), would be 'the worst possible plan'. In any government department it was essential that there should be one permanent head – thus any further separation must be at ministerial level.

Seely then attempted to strike a balance between setting up a separate office and leaving things as they were. If the British Government were free to do as it chose it would be a great deal better to leave well alone. First, the Colonial Office had been 'winning its way through its difficulties and . . . [was] . . . far less unpopular in the Dominions than it was forty, twenty, or even ten years ago'. Secondly, the 'principal advocates of change' – Deakin and Jameson – were out of office and thus would be absent from the Imperial Conference. And then there were the costs involved, including not less than £13,000 a year in additional salaries. Finally, there was much to be said for combining Dominion and crown colony work under the same departmental roof, for the problems to be solved were often the same in both, although the degree of Colonial Office control and influence naturally differed.

But against these considerations Seely thought that the British Government would probably be forced to make some change. The objection to the words 'Colonies' and 'Colonial' in the Dominions was very real and the feeling which gave rise to it was certain to grow rather than diminish. Moreover, the work of the Dominions Department seemed likely to expand, with the increasing interest of the Dominions in defence problems and the growing contact between Britain and the Dominions as a result of speedier travel and the growth of Dominion population and wealth.

Finally, Seely dealt with the question of the identity and title of the ministerial head of the new department. The assumption of responsibility by the Lord President, as suggested by Amery and Lucas, would have the advantage of not adding to the number of 'Principal Officers of State' but had the drawback of compelling the minister to be a member of the Lords, thus involving the Prime Minister as spokesman in the Commons. The title for the new department would be the 'Dominions Office' and its head might be called 'Secretary of State for the Dominions'. A 'most ingenious suggestion' had been made by a senior Colonial Office official that there should be a council of three, with the Prime Minister as president, the Secretary of State for the Dominions as vice-president and a 'member of council', who would be the equivalent of the Parliamentary Under-Secretary. The merit of this plan, Seely felt, was that although the new department would be set up on the well-established lines of other departments, 'in appearance the Prime Minister would be brought in as its head'. But, 'on full consideration', Seely doubted the wisdom of putting it forward. It would weaken the force of the argument that it was 'impossible for the Prime Minister of this country to give anything like the continuous personal attention even to the most important parts of the daily work of a Dominions Office'. The Dominion premiers might refuse the proposal when they realised that the Prime Minister would be only a figurehead. Once they had accepted that 'they cannot have the Prime Minister' the Dominion leaders would 'no doubt welcome the appointment of a separate Secretary of State for their affairs'.

The Parliamentary Under-Secretary at the Colonial Office was thus prepared to contemplate a separate Dominions Office, although reluctantly and in response to supposed Dominion demands rather than as a genuine administrative improvement. His ministerial chief, Harcourt, was, however, less flexible and faced the possibility of departmental reorganisation without the open mind that his predecessor as Colonial Secretary, Crewe, had been displaying towards the end of his tenure of office.

The Prime Minister (Asquith) and he, Harcourt wrote in his Cabinet paper of April 1911, shortly before the Imperial Conference assembled, had considered the proposals made by New Zealand and 'many other alternatives'.

They had come to the conclusion that at the Imperial Conference the least the Government could offer and the most it could give was a bifurcation of the Colonial Office at permanent under-secretary level (despite Seely's objections to this course), together with the addition to the conference secretariat of an advisory standing committee including Dominion representatives (an idea which had emerged from discussions with Sir Richard Solomon, the South African High Commissioner in London). The hope was that when the difficulties of bifurcation had been explained, the conference would reject it and accept instead the fairly innocuous standing committee as a kind of consolation prize. The British Government should not, Harcourt wrote, 'assent to the position of being told what the Dominions mean to ask and are prepared to accept . . . The acceptance of a spontaneous offer will look better than the acquiescence in a grudging compromise'.

Harcourt considered the arguments in favour of bifurcation to be of a 'purely sentimental nature' but 'for that reason must not be neglected'. Ministers of the 'younger' Dominions (by which Harcourt presumably meant all but Canada) appeared to feel some degradation in any association with the crown colonies, 'some of which were almost autonomous before the discovery of Australia or the civilisation of South Africa'. The demand was on grounds of 'social precedence' rather than 'administrative efficiency'.

The administrative objections to bifurcation raised in Harcourt's paper were in the main those he deployed to the Imperial Conference when it met in May 1911 (Cd. 5745): the difficulty of managing a department with dual permanent control (one man must be responsible for the overall control of the Office, and thus one permanent under-secretary would have to be senior to the other); the problem of dividing 'common service' departments such as the legal and accounts branches; and the desirability of co-ordinating policies between the two sides in one permanent head, for without this the 'common knowledge and power of correlation will reside only in the political chiefs, who are liable to change and leave no recorded experience to their successors'. But to the argument that Fiji, the Western Pacific islands and the South African High Commission Territories should be dealt with by the officials concerned with the Dominions, Harcourt added a prediction which was not mentioned at the conference. 'It appears almost certain', he wrote, 'that in a future not very remote the Dominions in temperate zones will desire to acquire for themselves "hot houses" for consumable luxuries and other purposes. It is not unreasonable to contemplate the ultimate absorption of the West Indies by Canada; of the Pacific islands by Australia and New Zealand; of Rhodesia and the native Protectorates (even of Nyasaland) by South Africa. But if the complete bifurcation of the Colonial Office is to be effected at once these Dominions will be divorced far more completely than at present from any knowledge of or interest in, or indirect influence over, their neighbouring Crown Colonies . . . under a system of absolute bifurcation I am convinced that they must be treated as Crown Colonies (which they are) and removed altogether from any Dominion control.'

Harcourt then turned to the question of ministerial responsibilities for Dominion affairs. The impossibility of the Prime Minister taking them over had already been emphasised at the 1907 conference and been tacitly accepted by it. Any arrangement whereby the Prime Minister was brought in as a figurehead in a 'bogus organisation' such as a council would soon be discovered to be a fraud and 'would cause more resentment in the Dominions than any satisfaction which might be created by the initial device'. The appointment of another minister, whether Lord President or a new Secretary of State, would entail the creation of a completely separate office, with a new Parliamentary Under-Secretary, and new legal and general branches, registry and library. An alternative suggestion was that, within a still integrated department, bifurcation might commence at the *Parliamentary* Under-Secretary level, with one Under-Secretary in the Commons and one in the Lords – but Harcourt saw no argument for this except 'the luxury' for the Secretary of State of always having a junior colleague in whichever House he happened to sit.

In the event, both the proposals put forward by the British Government at the 1911 conference – bifurcation of the Colonial Office and a standing committee to maintain continuity between conferences – proved unnecessary. Harcourt told the conference members that if they really pressed it and saw 'any advantage to themselves and to their Dominions from such a separation, we are willing to accept it and carry it out, though with some inconvenience, no doubt, in the office, which I will say no more about'. But the weight of opinion at the conference was against any fundamental change. Laurier gave no hint of his recent toying with the idea of a separate department and, aided by Botha of South Africa, was in fact at least as intractable a defender of the *status quo* as he had been at the 1907 conference. The absence of Deakin and Jameson undoubtedly had its effect, but perhaps even more influential were the misgivings aroused by the quasi-federal Imperial Council scheme incoherently presented by Ward of New Zealand, and roundly condemned by all his colleagues. This seemed to have created an atmosphere inimical to the serious consideration of more modest proposals. But whatever the cause, 'the Colonial Office emerged from the discussions unscathed', as A. B. Keith, who was junior assistant secretary at the conference, expressed it some years later, after he had left official for academic life (Keith, 1928, ii, 1187). Harcourt himself, who had explained to the conference that his proposals were a response to what the British Government felt the Dominions desired and did not represent any conscious want by that Government itself, was surprised at their lukewarm reception: he 'discovered to his astonishment that he was more colonial than the colonies' (Gladstone Papers, Add. MSS. 45992). Laurier spoke of the 'ample satisfaction' which the 1907 reorganisation had given in Canada, while F. S. Malan of South Africa also said that the changes then made 'worked very satisfactorily'. Even Sir Joseph Ward, although he had supported the standing committee as a step in the right direction, did so 'without in any way reflecting upon the work of the Colonial Office, because my experience has been that the work done by the Secretariat . . . has been done excellently'; and in his closing speech at the conference he went out of his way to praise the preliminary work by the Colonial Office, saying that he had 'never known work so well prepared, and so ready for the consideration of the members of the Conference'. Unlike the last Colonial Conference of 1907, the first Imperial Conference of 1911 had no organisational consequences for the conduct of Dominion business by the Colonial Office.

IV

Towards the Dominions Office

In 1911 the British Government had been prepared – if pressed by the Dominions – to divide the Colonial Office under two permanent heads, one for the Dominions and one for the crown colonies. Although this would not have involved a separate Dominions Office it would not have differed greatly from the 1925 change since the Dominions Office then set up continued to share minister and building with the Colonial Office. Why, then, did it take another fourteen years for the change to be made?

The answer is to be found mainly in the growth of alternative channels of communication, often by-passing the Colonial Office altogether, between the Dominion governments and United Kingdom Government departments. Dominion high commissioners – and all the Dominions apart from Newfoundland were represented in London by such officials by 1911 – provided perhaps the most frequently used alternative intermediary. They were in direct informal contact with individual Whitehall departments and thus in a good position to convey departmental views unofficially to their governments and *vice versa*. The Colonial Office, jealous of its position as the central British departmental contact for the Dominions, was concerned to prevent such by-passing, and at least three incidents early in 1911 involving the New Zealand

and South African high commissioners led to a re-appraisal of the position by the Colonial Office (C.O. 209/274, No. 8300; C.O. 532/35, No. 25309).

In a sense, direct communications through high commissioners struck at the *raison d'être* of the Colonial Office and its Dominions Department. 'We should not', one of its officials (Keith) minuted, 'unless and until it is decided that the Secretary of State's intervention is needless (in which case the Dominions Division of this Office would seem to be useless) pass unnoticed cases of direct communication.' Apart from the constitutional niceties of observing the position of both the Secretary of State and the Governor-General there were, the Colonial Office staff felt, positive administrative advantages in channelling through the Office. It had, or should have, more background information on policy questions and a wider view than a representative of one Dominion or of one British Government department possessed. Hartmann Just claimed that 'in all cases the action of the Colonial Office as an intermediary is to the advantage of the Dominion governments, as it is the duty and province of the Office to endeavour to attain the wishes of those governments, subject to due regard for the interests and principles involved'. Moreover, where questions involved more than one department 'there must be a correlating department – the Colonial Office is obviously the right department'.

As a result of the discussion a confidential circular letter was sent by Harcourt, the Colonial Secretary, to seven of his ministerial colleagues, including those at the Admiralty and the Post Office, which were recognised to be the 'worst offenders' among departments. The letter reminded its recipients that the Colonial Office should be the sole medium for communication between Dominion and Imperial governments except in 'cases of mere routine' or in any case in which the Colonial Secretary agreed special reasons made direct communication useful. In cases of doubt it was better to send the Office 'too much rather than too little'. But the trouble continued, especially from the 'worst offenders', and the Colonial Office seemed to be engaged in an unending struggle for procedural perfection.

Inevitably, with the increasing prominence of foreign policy and defence issues as the First World War approached, the Colonial Office became less important in these fields, and to at least one interested – if hardly impartial – observer (writing in the *Round Table*, iii, 590) it had become by 1913 merely 'a sorting office', with the most important aspects of Dominion affairs handled by other departments, especially the Foreign Office.

In the defence sphere the Committee of Imperial Defence, with its sub-committees and its secretariat, was playing an important role in the shaping of imperial defence policy, and the claim has been made that by 1911 its secretariat was replacing the Colonial Office as the channel of relations in defence matters (Johnson, 111). But although the Committee of Imperial Defence might take the lead in formulating policy proposals for discussion, it did not possess a channel of communication with the Dominions other than that provided by the Colonial Office, and there is no evidence of any direct approach between the Committee and the Dominions other than those occasions when Dominion ministers were in London. It seems doubtful whether the Committee fundamentally affected the channels of imperial communications before 1914 since the Dominion governments themselves, despite several invitations from the British Government, showed a marked reluctance to use its machinery (either because they were unwilling to be represented by their high commissioners or because they did not wish to be deprived of the services of a minister residing in London). Moreover, the Committee's position in the structure of British Government was by no means unequivocal. It was an advisory body to the Cabinet (or rather, to the Prime

Minister), with no mandatory or executive powers except as the Prime Minister and Cabinet might decide. Haldane, one of its main proponents, wrote quite clearly in 1911 that 'The Committee of Imperial Defence never touches policy. It ascertains facts and supplies technical information.' Asquith subsequently confirmed that 'no large question of policy was settled by the conclusions of the Committee of Imperial Defence'. The War Office and the Admiralty remained the principal formulators of defence policy, unco-ordinated though their plans often were (Mackintosh, 266, 272, 273). The Committee *informed* – and the Dominions were glad, when the opportunity arose (as it did in the three imperial sessions of the committee in May 1911, during the Imperial Conference), to avail themselves of information which had not, indeed, been vouchsafed to the British Cabinet as a whole at that time. Although these sessions were more valuable to the Dominions than the conference itself it is difficult not to believe that Asquith had his tongue at least partially in his cheek when he hailed them as a significant stage in the constitutional history of the empire. Britain's defence strategy required Dominion participation and it was politic to draw the Dominions into closer consultation on foreign and defence questions in order to secure it. But consultation and information fell far short of a share in policy formulation and in joint responsibility for the policy formulated – and Asquith was almost brutally frank in telling his Dominion colleagues at the 1911 conference that the British Government was not prepared to surrender to the Dominions any share in the control of the conduct of foreign policy. Nevertheless, had the 1911 experiment not been interrupted by the outbreak of war it is possible that imperial sessions of the Committee of Imperial Defence might have overshadowed the Imperial Conference proper in the same way as the wartime Imperial War Cabinets overshadowed the Imperial War Conferences (Tyler, 436). This could hardly have happened without some modification of the conference secretariat role of the Dominions Department of the Colonial Office.

When war came its exigencies eventually brought about what so many Dominion leaders had desired – a direct confrontation with the British Government, and in particular the Prime Minister. The Colonial Office became relatively less important as an intermediary, although it was by no means entirely superseded.

The next Imperial Conference was due in 1915 but it was not considered possible to hold it. Dominion ministers occasionally visited London and while there attended Cabinet meetings, but for continuous information on the progress of the war and transmission of their views to the British Government the Dominion governments at first had to rely on their high commissioners (in Canada's case he was also a member of the Canadian Cabinet) and on the Colonial Office machinery of surface letter and dispatch. This was not always satisfactory for their purposes and the memoirs of Sir Robert Borden, the Canadian Prime Minister throughout the war, record numerous examples of lack of consultation in the years 1915 and 1916. Some improvement in information was effected when Walter Long became Colonial Secretary at the end of 1916 for he instituted a weekly telegram to the Dominions on the war situation and prospects, by which 'they were put in possession every Tuesday morning of everything of importance that we knew on the Monday' (Long, 237). In 1917 a more important development took place. It was decided – apparently as a result of pressure by L. S. Amery and Lord Milner, a member of the War Cabinet – to hold an Imperial War Conference on the lines of the pre-war Imperial Conference, but to have simultaneously with it – in alternate sessions – something rather inexactly termed the 'Imperial War Cabinet', consisting of the British War Cabinet and the Dominion Prime Ministers attending the conference; the Imperial War Cabinet dealing with the actual conduct of the war, the Imperial War Conference dealing with the more general inter-imperial questions (Amery, ii, 91). Although the Imperial War Cabinet and Conferences were not a continuous machinery (assembling for two separate periods in 1917 and 1918) they at least operated more frequently, for a longer period, and in a more definite field, than the pre-war quadrennial conferences, and gave the Dominion ministers a real insight into wartime policy formulation.

The new wartime system of Cabinet and conference ended permanently the Colonial Office's monopoly in the provision of the conference secretariat. The Imperial War Cabinet was serviced by the new British War Cabinet secretariat, assisted by the head of the Dominions Department; it was only for the less important War Conferences that the Dominions Department was responsible for providing the secretariat. It is significant that at the first of the post-war Imperial Conferences (although officially it did not rank as one) – in 1921 – the four-man United Kingdom contingent on the inter-Dominion conference secretariat under the Secretary to the British Cabinet (Hankey) had only one Colonial Office representative, and the dominant position of the Cabinet secretariat was maintained for the 1923 conference and all subsequent Imperial Conferences. The 1907 secretariat had clearly become moribund, and no mention of its members was made in the *Colonial Office List* after 1921. The *ad hoc* inter-Dominion secretariats which succeeded it provided a part of what Deakin and others had wanted in 1907 – Dominion representation – but at the expense of that continuity which they had also felt to be important and which, however imperfectly in their eyes, the Dominions Department had provided.

Another legacy of the wartime system was the initiation, at the 1918 Imperial War Conference, of direct communication between Dominion premiers and the British Prime Minister. The discussion which preceded the passing of the resolution, in which W. M. Hughes, Prime Minister of Australia, played a leading part, clearly linked the new departure with the continuing dissatisfaction with the Colonial Office-Governor-General channel (Fiddes, 263–4). In the Imperial War Cabinet, Hughes declared, all intermediaries had been swept away and government met government face to face. A situation had developed for which the old methods of communication were no longer appropriate. The division of the Colonial Office into Dominion and crown colony branches was good as far as it went, but the change must go deeper. As regards the Dominions the Colonial Office had become 'an anachronism' and its functions were 'merely those of an unnecessary conduit pipe'. Dominions correspondence should go direct to the Prime Minister, possibly with an assistant minister to relieve him of unnecessary duties. But what was immediately necessary, Hughes declared, was that when a Dominion Prime Minister was negotiating with the British Prime Minister he should be able to confer with him directly and not through the mediation of another British minister.

The other members of the conference, while welcoming direct communication between Prime Ministers, dissociated this from any criticism of recent Colonial Secretaries or the work of the Colonial Office. Massey, Prime Minister of New Zealand, encouragingly, if somewhat obscurely, described the Colonial Office as having done 'well, thoroughly and enthusiastically'. Cook, the Australian Minister of the Navy, confessed to an occasion when his department had ignored the Colonial Office channel but had had to return to it and secured 'prompt dispatch'; he thought that as a good deal of Dominion correspondence was hardly appropriate to the British Prime Minister, the channel of communications in such matters might very well remain where it was. Borden of Canada pointed out the undesirability of imposing on the British Prime Minister duties which he could only nominally discharge.

Ward, who had been New Zealand Prime Minister at the 1907 and 1911 conferences and was now Minister of Finance, thought it quite impossible for the British Prime Minister to undertake 'the great and varied work' which the Colonial Office had been doing over the years.

Although it may have had a certain symbolic value the system of direct communication between Prime Ministers seems in practice to have proved less important than had been expected (Palmer, 19; C.O. 537/1035). It was used sparingly, and mainly for telegrams involving major foreign policy issues which, until the end of the Lloyd George Coalition Government, tended to be concentrated in the hands of the Prime Minister rather than the Foreign Office. On other matters there was an informal arrangement between No. 10, Downing Street and the Colonial Office whereby the Colonial Office itself took the necessary action, drafting the Prime Minister's communications and submitting them for his approval, if considered necessary. They were then sent via the Colonial Office–Governor-General channel in the same way as other communications between the British and Dominion governments.

The 1918 conference also provided for the transmission to the Dominions of 'important papers pertinent to the business of the Imperial War Cabinet', when that body was not in session. The practice was confirmed in 1919, and in 1921 provision was made for a much more comprehensive service of Foreign Office confidential telegrams and Cabinet papers which until then had been seen only by the British Cabinet and British missions abroad. The Foreign Office made the selection, the Colonial Office again being responsible for dispatching the material. In the event, the supply of such information proved 'meagre', and the Colonial Office had several times to remind the Foreign Office of its obligations under the 1921 arrangement (C.O. 537/1035). Moreover, the material was sent by surface mail and was thus subject to considerable delay.

43

Normally this was of no great moment, but it was clearly unsatisfactory at periods of crisis: no reports had been received in Canada, for example, in the ten days which preceded the British Government telegram requesting Dominion help in the Chanak crisis in September 1922 (Eayrs, 131).

But however sparing the use made of the direct Prime Minister channel the fact that it existed at all had clear implications for the traditional Colonial Office link through the Governor-General. The war and its aftermath – Dominion participation in the peace-making at Versailles and their individual entry into membership of the League of Nations – had developed their national status in the international sphere. The necessity of defeating a common enemy had produced an ultimately illusory unity of purpose during the war, for Lloyd George's attempt to continue the Imperial War Cabinet system in peacetime was early doomed to failure. No longer were the Dominions prepared automatically to follow the foreign policy initiatives of the British Government; the 'diplomatic unity of the British Empire' was, in practical terms, at an end. In these circumstances the role of the Governor-General as both an agent of the Colonial Office and the formal representative of the Crown was becoming increasingly anomalous. As long ago as 1910 J. C. Smuts had visualised the Crown, rather than a British Government representative, as the link between the autonomous countries of the empire, and he returned to the theme in memoranda of 1919 and 1921. And the continuance of the Governor-General channel was not helped by its obvious inadequacies at times of crisis: the Chanak telegram, received at the Governor-General's office in Ottawa at 10 p.m. on 15th September (1922), was not delivered to Mackenzie King, the Canadian Prime Minister, until 3 p.m. on 16th September – two hours after the news had appeared in the Canadian press, a fact which did not assist its favourable reception by the Canadian Government (Eayrs, 29). The ground was being prepared for the Imperial Conference resolution of 1926.

Although the Colonial Office was thus becoming relatively less important in the process of inter-governmental communications, the question of departmental reorganisation was not entirely lost sight of. Suggestions for the creation of a separate Dominions department or for the re-allocation of ministerial responsibilities, or both, continued to be made during and after the war (Pugh, 1959, 758). They were put forward in the British Parliament, for example, in 1916 and 1917, and parliamentary agitation for such a change increased from 1919 onwards, much of it motivated by a desire to free the Colonial Office from its Dominion responsibilities so that it could concentrate on the task of developing the colonies rather than solely to recognise the national status of the Dominions. Sometimes the Prime Minister, sometimes the Lord President, was proposed as the ideal minister to handle Dominion affairs, but the suggestions were all rejected by the Government, as was the later, more modest, suggestion that the title of the Colonial Secretary should be changed. In its defence the Government was able to point to the fact that, since the discussion on channels of communication at the 1918 conference, there had been no formal representations on the subject of Colonial Office reorganisation by the Dominions themselves. Thus, when the announcement of the reorganisation eventually came in 1925, it could be claimed that it was on the initiative of the British Government, although, of course, there had been consultations with the Dominion governments, and they had welcomed the proposed change (Fiddes, 277). The man mainly responsible for the reorganisation, L. S. Amery, explained the lack of Dominion initiative as being 'not so much because the position has been regarded as satisfactory as because the Dominions have felt it hardly consistent with the principles on which inter-Imperial relations are based to go beyond a certain

45

point in expressing their views as to the internal administration and organisation of another part of the Empire'
(187 H.C.Deb., col 68). That at least one distinguished
imperial statesman was still interested in British departmental organisation Amery knew from his correspondence
in June 1921 with Smuts, over the latter's private memorandum on imperial relations (Hall, 1962, 175, 179).
Smuts envisaged that the Dominions, as co-ordinate
governments of the King with full equality of status,
'would cease to be placed under the Colonial Office or
any other British department'. Amery told him that he
agreed Dominions work should be taken away from the
Colonial Office, but he foresaw that there would still be
a need 'for some central office to deal with Dominion
matters affecting a number of British departments'. Nevertheless it is unlikely that the subject provoked as much
interest in the Dominions as in the days of Deakin. A
degree of apathy over something that was no longer considered by the Dominions to be of fundamental importance would seem to be a likelier explanation of their lack
of initiative in the matter than unwillingness to hurt the
feelings of the British Government.

When, on 6th November, 1924, it was announced that
L. S. Amery was to be Colonial Secretary in the new
Baldwin administration it was clear that a change could
not be long delayed. No doubt sensing this, *The Times*
on 11th November urged the new minister (who had once
been a *Times* leader-writer) to declare that the time was
ripe for the frank recognition that his department was
not the proper channel for Dominion liaison. This was
preaching to the converted for, as we have seen, Amery
had long been a critic of Colonial Office responsibility for
Dominion affairs. His tour of East Africa in 1907–8 and
his earlier experience at the Colonial Office as Parliamentary Under-Secretary (1919–21) had convinced him
that both sides of the work – Dominion and colonial –
suffered from being performed in the same department.

In accepting the Colonial Secretaryship he had stipulated to Baldwin that he 'should be allowed to create a new and entirely separate office to deal with the Dominions', for he regarded it as indispensable to 'any fruitful development' in United Kingdom-Dominion relations that the British Government should give a clear indication that it considered the essentially diplomatic task of dealing with the Dominion governments as 'wholly different in character from the administration of the dependent Empire' (Amery, 1953, ii, 335).

Amery had no difficulty in proving to his colleagues that, quite apart from the political reasons for dividing the Office, the growth of the work on both sides fully justified the change. The aftermath of the war had enormously increased the volume of correspondence with the Dominions (which now included the Irish Free State), and in addition there were the wholly new series of negotiations involved in giving effect to the Empire Settlement Act of 1921 (providing Government assistance for emigration to the Dominions). On the other hand the task of colonial administration was not only growing all the time, but now also included an entirely new field in Palestine, Transjordan and Iraq, which had been mandated to Britain under the peace treaty.

Nevertheless, it was not until 11th June, 1925 – eight months after Amery had taken office – that the announcement of the proposed establishment of a separate Dominions Office was made by the Prime Minister (184 H.C.Deb., cols. 2239–40). The matter had been held up, according to Amery, by the determination of the Treasury to save £800 a year on the salary of the new Permanent Under-Secretary, compared with his counterparts in other departments. The Treasury won, after 'months of argument', interrupted by Amery's visit to the Middle East in March-April 1925, but even after the announcement on 11th June things were not completely settled and Amery (who was to hold the two appointments) had to kiss hands

47

on appointment as Secretary of State for Dominion Affairs in some haste the next month to avoid the necessity of facing the by-election then required by the Re-election of Ministers Act, 1919 (Amery, 1953, ii, 336).

Both Baldwin's announcement and Amery's elaboration of it a few weeks later (187 H.C. Deb., cols. 67–70), stressed the differences between the nature of the departmental work involved in Dominion relations, on the one hand, and colonial administration on the other. Baldwin spoke of the existing organisation of the Colonial Office being no longer 'in correspondence with the actual constitutional position in the Empire' and 'inadequate to the extent and variety of the work thrown upon it'. The two spheres of work – Dominion and colonial – differed, Amery said, not merely in degree but in kind. The former function was 'political, consultative . . . quasi-diplomatic' (from the Opposition benches Runciman referred to the new Office as 'a Foreign Office with a family feeling'); the latter, 'administrative and directive'. They called, he thought, 'for wholly different methods and qualities of mind.' It was 'the consciousness of this difference, and the feeling that it was not always adequately recognised, which more than any mere sentimental objection to the word Colonial, has always created a certain amount of resentment in the Dominions against the idea that their relations with the Mother Country should be dealt with by the Colonial Office'. In this connection, Amery recalled his friend Deakin's 'eloquent and forcible appeal for a better arrangement of our work in dealing with the Dominions' at the 1907 conference. It was indeed appropriate that the man who had exerted the greatest individual influence from the British side on the development of British departmental organisation for Dominion relations should thus pay tribute to his Dominion counterpart (who had died six years before).

The change was generally welcomed, but A. B. Keith, who had worked in the Dominions Department for the

first seven years of its existence, was something less than
enthusiastic about the way in which it was effected. He
believed that Amery's retention of both offices 'caused
a painful impression in Dominion circles, suggesting that
the change was due to personal considerations rather than
grounds of state' (Keith, ii, 915). Keith's theory (which
could conceivably have been based on Office 'gossip') was
that the burden of his duties as head of an Office with
greatly-increased responsibilities was proving too severe
for Amery and when, in 1925, the Permanent Under-
Secretaryship had to be filled, he was unable to promote
one of the staff, and solved the impasse by dividing the
Office, appointing an outsider (with, however, much
colonial experience) to the Colonial division and a member of the staff to the Dominions division. The first Permanent Under-Secretary at the Dominions Office was,
however, Sir Charles Davis (the head of the Dominions
Department), an old college friend of Amery, who speaks
highly of him in his autobiography. If there were any
doubts about his fitness to be permanent head of the un-
divided Office they were more likely to be on grounds
of his health, which was poor, than of his competence.
It would seem virtually certain that the separation of the
offices came at this particular juncture because of Amery's
assumption of the Colonial Secretaryship. Even if the
experience of office had acquainted him with any administrative difficulties there might be in such a change he
could hardly have avoided making it, when given the
opportunity, in view of his past advocacy. There is no
reason to believe that Amery was reluctant to be in a
position to achieve such a long-standing objective.

V

From Dominions Office to Commonwealth Relations Office

In practice the creation of the Dominions Office did not involve any really fundamental change in administrative organisation. While the new department had its own parliamentary Vote and separate Parliamentary and Permanent Under-Secretaries (unlike its Dominions Department predecessor), for several years it shared its responsible minister with the Colonial Office, together with the same building in Downing Street, establishments (below assistant under-secretary level), registry, legal staff, library, accounts and printing. It thus did not provide the separate roof and separate minister considered desirable by Lord Grey and Sir Charles Lucas, for example, and represented both more and less than was envisaged in the 1911 Cabinet papers of Seely and Harcourt. Seely's projected Dominions Office was to provide all its own services except for the library and printing; and Harcourt, possibly to ensure (or in the hope) that the idea would be rejected, had adumbrated a wholly separate department, with no common branches. The 1925 change – at least while the two Offices were headed by the same minister (1925–30 and for short periods in 1931 and 1938–9) – was more akin to the offer of bifurcation actually made to the 1911 conference than the establishment of an independent department. Moreover, it would not have escaped attention in Whitehall, where status and salary so often go together, that the new Permanent Under-Secretary received considerably less salary than his Colonial Office colleague (and continued to do so until 1940).

The Dominions Office, under the Secretary of State and his Parliamentary Under-Secretary, was originally divided into three departments, each headed by an assistant secretary (Fiddes, 280–1). Above this grade there was an assistant under-secretary and the Permanent Under-Secretary, each of whom exercised a general supervision. The departments were organised partly on a subject, and partly on a geographical, basis. One department dealt with such questions as foreign affairs, defence, consular and general passport matters, cables and wireless, honours and ceremonies, and the combined United Kingdom-Australian-New Zealand mandated territory of Nauru; the second department, with Canada, the Irish Free State and Newfoundland, economic questions, naturalisation, and merchant shipping; while the third department dealt with the Australian Commonwealth and States, New Zealand, South Africa, Southern Rhodesia (self-governing since 1923, but not a Dominion), the South African High Commission Territories, and Asiatic questions. In addition, there was an Overseas Settlement Department (the successor of the Emigrants' Information Office established in 1886) which, while physically separate from the Dominions Office, carried on its functions of assisting emigration to Commonwealth countries as a department of the Office.

The one obvious anomaly in this allocation of functions – and it went back to the Dominions Department of 1907 – was the assignment of the High Commission Territories of Basutoland, Bechuanaland and Swaziland to the Dominions Office rather than to the Colonial Office, to which, as colonies, they properly belonged. The other colonial territories with which the Dominions Department had dealt because of their contiguity to Dominions – Fiji and the Western Pacific islands – did remain with the

Colonial Office after 1925. The assumption which under-lay the special departmental treatment for the High Commission Territories was the possibility that the territories might eventually be transferred to South Africa: it was only when South Africa left the Commonwealth in 1961 that the affairs of the territories were transferred back to the Colonial Office.

The Dominions Office was initially very small, containing only thirteen administrative class officials (Permanent Under-Secretary, assistant under-secretary, three assistant secretaries, four principals and four assistant principals) and eighteen other staff, most of them being registry clerks (*Dominions Office and Colonial Office List*). On such a restricted scale it could hardly have enjoyed an independent existence but for the services provided for it by the Colonial Office.

By 1938 the administrative and other staff had more than doubled. Under the Permanent Under-Secretary there were now two assistant under-secretaries (the second having been appointed in 1931), five assistant secretaries (each in charge of a department), thirteen principals, ten assistant principals and thirty-eight other staff. Although the departmental organisation still had a geographical element it had been considerably reduced since 1925. Department A dealt with constitutional and nationality questions, Ireland, ceremonial and honours, civil aviation, and establishments; Department B with defence, imperial communications, broadcasting, bilateral non-League of Nations conventions, and the Arctic and Antarctic; Department C with international economic questions, imperial economic relations, intra-imperial trade agreements, and shipping; Department D with Newfoundland (which had ceased to be a Dominion, at its own request), the British Phospate Commission (operating in the mandated territory of Nauru), Southern Rhodesia, and the High Commission Territories; and Department E with migration (the Oversea Settlement Department had been disbanded) and miscellaneous questions. Thus no department dealt with the 'Old Dominions' – Canada, Australia, New Zealand and South Africa – as such: their business was distributed throughout the five, predominantly 'subject' departments.

The most important development which had taken place since 1925 was the creation of a Dominions Office overseas service, staffing the offices of United Kingdom high commissioners in the Dominions, the first of whom (the High Commissioner to Canada) had been appointed in 1928. One of the commonest criticisms made by the Dominions of the Colonial Office when it was still departmentally responsible for their affairs was that its staff lacked personal knowledge of Dominion conditions. Occasionally senior members would visit Dominions (as they did to Canada in 1910 and to Australia and New Zealand in 1909 and 1914), and occasionally also junior members were attached to the staff of a Governor-General. But, in general, as someone who entered it in 1909 observed, 'The most serious defect of the Colonial Office at this time was lack of local knowledge and "background" so invaluable to anyone working in Whitehall' (Parkinson, 46). The Office's official link with and source of information on the Dominions were the Governors-General, who combined the functions of head of state and British 'diplomatic' representative. Their usefulness in the latter role depended on their perspicacity and the intimacy of their relationship with the Dominion government concerned. On the whole, Dominion governments were reluctant to take the Governor-General into their confidence, largely because he was primarily an official appointed by another government for that government's purposes.

As we have seen in Chapter IV, the Governor-General's position was becoming increasingly anomalous as the Dominions became more obviously independent states in practice. In 1926 the 'Byng Affair' in Canada – which in fact occurred after the Governor-General (Lord Byng) had exercised his function as head of state (in refusing Mackenzie King's request for a dissolution) rather than as British Government representative – prompted Mackenzie King to have the whole question of the role of the Governor-General aired at the Imperial Conference of that year. The final report of that conference declared that the Governor-General was His Majesty's representative in a Dominion (thus a head of state only, not a British Government representative) and provided for direct communication between the British Government (through the Dominions Office) and the Dominion governments, by-passing the Governor-General, for any Dominion which wished it. Canada availed itself of the opportunity almost immediately (1927), and the other Dominions followed suit, New Zealand in 1941 being the last to abandon the old system (Eayrs, 30).

But intimate relations between governments as closely associated as were the United Kingdom and Dominion governments could not exist merely on the exchange of official dispatches. Since the Governor-General could no longer speak for the British Government in a Dominion capital, a new channel for private, personal communication was required. In London itself there were the Dominion high commissioners, and some of the Dominion premiers argued that official dispatches could be supplemented by collective private discussions between the high commissioners and the Foreign Office or Dominions Office. But Mackenzie King, who had a deep and ineradicable suspicion that consultation and discussion might be interpreted as commitment to British policies, was not prepared to allow his high commissioner to take part in such private discussions (Eayrs, 131–2; Massey, 236). If the Canadian Prime Minister could deal with an agent of the British Government in *Canada*, however, he would be able to form his own opinions and determine the exact wording of his reply. It was Mackenzie King who was instrumental in securing the appointment to Canada of the first United Kingdom High Commissioner in 1928 (Neatby, 188); similar appointments were subsequently made to the other Dominions, New Zealand being the last in this development – as in other Commonwealth developments – when a high commissioner was appointed there in 1939.

United Kingdom high commissioners were not always recruited from the Dominions Office – occasionally they came from the ranks of politicians or from other departments – but their subordinate staff came, for the most part, from the Office. Thus of the thirteen principals in 1938, three were serving in the Dominions. The Office had now, for the first time, assumed an explicitly representational role, and one which was to increase *pari passu* with the expansion of the British Commonwealth of Nations (as the Dominions and Britain were collectively known from about the end of the 1914–18 war) and the increasingly complex character of international affairs. But unlike the Foreign Office staff, members of the Dominions Office remained in the home civil service, and were recruited as such. They were thus selected on their potential as administrators rather than as diplomats, even though the appointment entailed a liability to serve overseas, where their duties would be predominantly diplomatic in character (Mansergh, 1958, 399). There is no evidence to suggest, however, that the staff of high commissions were any less skilful diplomats than their Foreign Office counterparts. As time went on members of the Foreign Service were occasionally seconded to high commissions, as were members of the Dominions Office staff to foreign missions.

The outbreak of war in 1939 – a war in which all the Dominions apart from Eire participated – inevitably widened and deepened the scope of Commonwealth consultation and co-operation. The process had in fact been speeded up with the immediate pre-war crises, beginning

E

with the Italian invasion of Abyssinia in 1935. London was the centre of this consultation and the key elements in the machinery were the Dominions Office and – despite Mackenzie King's dislike of consultations beyond his immediate control – the Dominion high commissioners in London, one of the most distinguished of whom (Vincent Massey, of Canada) has given his account of the process in his memoirs (*What's Past is Prologue*). During the last months of 1935 and throughout 1936 the Dominion high commissioners as a group met the Dominions Secretary frequently to discuss the Abyssinian and Rhineland crises. The Munich crisis of September 1938 again led to frequent such meetings, which sometimes took place more than once on the same day.

The high commissioners' meetings with the Dominions Secretary continued after the outbreak of war, but with a greatly altered character. They met daily, sometimes including Sundays, with the Dominions Secretary and the Parliamentary and Permanent Under-Secretaries, and heard important Foreign Office telegrams and military reports; occasionally the Foreign Secretary joined them to explain matters of special importance. The high commissioners could not commit their governments (Mackenzie King, if no other Dominion premier, would not have tolerated this) but they were able to say what attitude their countries would be likely to take towards specific issues as they arose. They were encouraged to give their personal views and often did so.

The usefulness of the meetings depended on a two-way process – a flow of essential secret information about the conduct of the war from the Dominions Secretary and an effective channelling by him of the high commissioners' views to the policy-making machine. This process depended in turn on the personality of the Dominions Secretary and his status in the Government. Whereas Eden, Dominions Secretary from 1939 to 1940, was 'admirable' (according to Vincent Massey) his successor, Lord Caldecote, was 'not sufficiently close to the centre of the stage to enable the high commissioners to function to the best of their abilities'. Lord Cranborne was an 'admirable choice' to succeed Caldecote in October 1940 but even his 'very great ability could not compensate for his exclusion from the inner circle', as a consequence of which the quality of information put at the disposal of the high commissioners continued to deteriorate. The trouble was in part due to the fact that the Dominions Secretary, apart from the period from February 1942 to September 1943, was not a member of the War Cabinet. He usually attended War Cabinet meetings, but this was not the same thing – and even this privilege was curtailed on occasion, as when Cranborne told the high commissioners in November 1941 that henceforth he was to be allowed to attend only one of the two weekly meetings of the War Cabinet. Moreover, when the Dominions Secretary – in the person of C. R. Attlee – *was* a full member of the War Cabinet (1942–3) he was 'unduly reluctant' in passing on information to the high commissioners. Australia, which perhaps felt its geographical isolation from the centres of strategic policy-making more than the other Dominions, requested, and eventually (June 1942) secured, the right of its High Commissioner (S. M. Bruce, himself a former Prime Minister) to attend War Cabinet meetings himself. But according to his Canadian colleague, Massey, this concession did not add greatly to Bruce's knowledge of the conduct of the war, or to that of his fellow high commissioners. If high commissioners were excluded from the inner circle, so apparently were members of the War Cabinet itself.

The Prime Minister (Churchill) was in fact disinclined, apparently largely on security grounds, to divulge important information to the Dominions. In a directive to the Dominions Secretary in December 1940 he instructed the Office 'not to scatter so much deadly and secret information over this very large circle'. While there should be no change in principle in the channelling of information to the Dominions, 'there should be considerable soft-pedalling in practice'. Later in the war a Dominions Office official complained to Massey of Churchill's failure to use the experience and knowledge of the Office in his relations with Dominion governments. Nevertheless information on international affairs did go out in considerable bulk to the Dominions, the Dominions Office working in close co-operation with the Commonwealth Liaison Department of the Foreign Office to process for Dominion consumption material derived from Foreign Office telegrams to British overseas missions. By the end of the war something like 23,000 telegrams a year were being handled by the Dominions Office, while the number of circular telegrams sent to the Dominions was almost quadrupled between 1937 and 1947 (Mansergh, 1958, 401).

At the higher levels of wartime governmental consultation there was no counterpart to the Imperial War Cabinet and Conferences of 1917 and 1918. But, as in the First World War, Dominion ministers visiting London frequently attended meetings of the War Cabinet, and in May 1944 a conference which later came to be seen as the first of the still-continuing series of Meetings of Commonwealth Prime Ministers was held in London. This, to quote from the New Zealand Prime Minister's subsequent report to his Parliament, expressed 'general satisfaction . . . at the measure of co-operation and consultation already established'. A new development resulting from this conference was the institution of a monthly meeting of Dominion high commissioners with the Prime Minister, to supplement the daily conferences at the Dominions Office (Mansergh, 1952, i, 593–4); it is significant, however, that no mention of this new provision is made in Vincent Massey's informed account of wartime Dominion consultation in London, and it may well be that the meetings never became fully established.

The expansion in the activities of the Dominions Office

resulting from wartime exigencies was not arrested with the arrival of peace. The Office was soon departmentally involved, along with the India Office, in the prolonged negotiations which eventually led to the independence of India and Pakistan as members of the Commonwealth in August 1947. Earlier in the same year, 1947, the Colonial Office moved out into other office accommodation, leaving the Dominions Office in sole possession of the office in Downing Street. At the same time the joint establishment with the Colonial Office came to an end. The re-naming of the Office as the 'Commonwealth Relations Office' in July 1947 was thus more than just a change in terminology – it represented, so to speak, a departmental coming of age. Moreover, the next month (August) its responsibilities were greatly augmented as a result of the abolition of the India Office and the transfer of departmental oversight of Britain's relations with the newly-independent India and Pakistan to the C.R.O. The merger was not, however, without its difficulties. Many of the India Office staff were under no obligation to serve overseas (the Indian Civil Service had been completely separate from the India Office), whereas Dominions Office staff had always – at least since 1928 – accepted this obligation as part of their duties. In addition, there was the problem of incorporating senior India Office officials into an already existing C.R.O. hierarchy. For a year or more the two departments continued to exist side by side, the C.R.O. as Division A and the former India Office as Division B, each complete with Permanent Under-Secretary and subordinate officials: the result was later pungently described by General Sir Archibald Nye, who was serving as British High Commissioner in India at the time, as 'a complete dog's breakfast' (Estimates Committee Report, 1959, 121). It was not until January 1949 that the Office reverted to having one Permanent Under-Secretary, and it was some months after that before the merger was finally completed.

Even after the absorption of the India Office the C.R.O. remained a relatively small department. In 1956 – the year before the admission to independent membership of the Commonwealth of Ghana and Malaya (the first new members since India, Pakistan and Ceylon in 1947–8) – administrative staff totalled only 135, seventy of them serving in the Office in London, and sixty-five in the various United Kingdom posts in Commonwealth countries (Mackenzie and Grove, 225). Superimposed on the traditional departmental structure (under assistant secretaries) was now a series of divisions, each under an assistant under-secretary of state. The principle of organisation was predominantly functional in appearance, with Establishments and Organisation, Foreign Affairs, Economic, and Political Divisions. The one geographical division was the Africa and General, added after the formation of the Federation of Rhodesia and Nyasaland in 1953. But the actual distribution of the departments within the divisions gave a very much less clearcut picture. The Foreign Affairs Division was sub-divided geographically into Far Eastern, South Asian and Middle Eastern, Western and United Nations departments, and also included the Defence and Principal Staff Officer's departments. The Political Division, belying its name, was really a 'miscellaneous' division, with Constitutional, Communications, and Protocol and Nationality departments, the Library and the India Office Library. The one geographical division – Africa and General – contained functional departments in the Information and Cultural Relations department (which became a division in its own right in 1959), Migration, and General departments. When Ghana and Malaya business was transferred from the Colonial Office to the C.R.O. in the following year (1957) it was not distributed among existing departments but given to newly-established Ghana and Malaya departments within the Political Division, although this division was by 1959 shorn of its miscellaneous responsibilities (which were absorbed by the

Establishments and Organisation Division) and as a result consisted of the two new departments, together with the Constitutional department.

This rather complex organisational pattern was subjected to critical examination when the Select Committee on Estimates for the 1958–59 parliamentary session came to investigate the C.R.O. Estimates for that year. The then Permanent Under-Secretary, Sir Gilbert Laithwaite, explained that the Office had been organised on a functional basis in 1947 but it had not worked completely satisfactorily and experiments with alternative methods continued to be made. He thought it possible that with further experience there would be a greater emphasis on the geographical principle. But the present system was 'completely flexible'.

The Estimates Committee, understandably, was not entirely convinced by this explanation, and in particular questioned whether the addition of new Commonwealth members could simply, as in the case of Ghana and Malaya, be met by the expedient of creating departments specifically to deal with their affairs. An informal organisation might work in a small department, responsible for Britain's relations with a relatively confined group of countries, for it is relatively easy in these circumstances for officials to know all their colleagues personally and keep in touch with general Commonwealth developments. But as the number of countries with which the C.R.O. had to deal increased this would no longer be the case, and the Estimates Committee doubted whether the existing system of organisation, despite the flexibility claimed for it, was 'conducive to efficiency in administration'.

Some attention seems to have been paid to the committee's report since three years later (1962) – when several more countries, particularly in Africa, had achieved independence – the organisation of the Office presented a much more orderly appearance. Within the six divisions the departments were arranged more coherently: the

Africa Division, for example, now had three departments, each dealing with particular African regions, while the Political Division comprised Constitutional and General departments only. By the beginning of 1966 even more radical changes had been made and the divisions – now increased to eight – were divided between four geographical divisions (Asia and Atlantic, Central Africa, East and West Africa, and Far East and Mediterranean) and four subject divisions (Defence and Commonwealth Policy, General, Information, and Trade). The great increase in the work of the Office in recent years was reflected in its top échelons: a Minister of State was now regularly appointed to assist the Secretary of State and, at the official level, there were three deputy under-secretaries under the Permanent Under-Secretary, while the number of assistant under-secretaries (which in the Dominions Office had, until 1939, been the most senior rank below the Permanent Under-Secretary) ran into double figures.

Organisationally the pre-war Dominions Office was hardly recognisable in the modern Commonwealth Relations Office. But there still remained a similarity of approach to Commonwealth relations between the two Offices – an approach which, indeed, went back to the Dominions Department of the Colonial Office. As long ago as 1910 Hartmann Just wrote of the Colonial Office 'policy of non-interference and not forcing the pace' in relation to the Dominions. This remained the cardinal principle of Commonwealth relations two generations later. One of the major concerns of the C.R.O., as of its predecessors, was to avoid giving offence to Britain's Commonwealth partners and this meant that its activities were more emollient than dynamic : its officials, to quote Just's 1910 memorandum again, necessarily worked 'in the shade' and eschewed 'exceptional and increased activity'.

A recent official description of the functions of the C.R.O. would have fitted, more or less accurately, the pre-war Dominions Office. They consist in :

(i) advising ministers on every aspect of British policy likely to affect other members of the Commonwealth;

(ii) co-ordinating the views of the various British departments on the policies of other Commonwealth countries insofar as they affect British interests;

(iii) arranging consultations with the other members of the Commonwealth on all matters of common concern; and

(iv) acting as the main channel through which information and statements of policy are sent to and received from other Commonwealth countries on all subjects of mutual interest, such as foreign policy, defence co-operation, and economic and social welfare. (*The Future of the Commonwealth*, 27.)

The Office is thus not merely a 'post office' between the overseas Commonwealth countries and British Government departments. It does more than pass on information – it has the job of advising the Cabinet on all policy matters which concern other members of the Commonwealth, regardless of which British Government department is departmentally responsible for the policy. The Commonwealth Secretary is, in fact, one of the fairly select band of ministers who have always been included in the Cabinet. Moreover, the C.R.O.'s control over the British representational staff in Commonwealth countries means that it controls also the machinery through which other British departments normally communicate with Commonwealth governments (Miller, 1960-1, 46). The British high commissioners in Commonwealth countries are indeed the key figures in the normal process of British consultation with the overseas Commonwealth. There are other avenues at a higher level – such as meetings of Prime Ministers and other ministers – but these are intermittent. The high commissioner link is continuously in use, and often in a way much less formal, more widely pervasive and in greater depth than an embassy in a foreign country (as Lord Amory, a recent high commissioner himself, described it in the 1964 Lords debate on the Plowden Report).

The Commonwealth Relations Office was thus both a product of the uniqueness of the Commonwealth relationship and a contributor to the usefulness of the association. This meant that the continuing development of the Commonwealth, the changes in the number and outlook of its members, could not leave the Office unaffected.

VI

Recent Developments

Since 1965 the Commonwealth Relations Office has undergone significant changes. It has developed much closer organisational links with the Foreign Office and has absorbed the Colonial Office (becoming the 'Commonwealth Office' in the process). And outside the sphere of British departmental organisation for Commonwealth relations, but impinging upon it, there is now a truly Commonwealth Secretariat.

i Full Circle – the Formation of the Commonwealth Office

At the time of the Dominions Office's metamorphosis into the Commonwealth Relations Office in 1947 its sister department the Colonial Office was overwhelmingly the more important, with responsibility for the vast dependent empire of the United Kingdom. Asian independence in 1947-8 affected Colonial Office functions only to the extent of the transfer of Ceylon to the C.R.O., since India and Burma had always been in other departmental hands. In 1947, too, although a move towards developing self-governing institutions in the dependencies was clearly discernible, few could have predicted the impetus it would gather in the course of the next ten or fifteen years. But the attainment of internal self-government by the Gold

Coast in 1951 gave an indication of what was in store, and this was made fully manifest with the full independence, as members of the Commonwealth, of Ghana (the former Gold Coast) and Malaya in 1957 and the independence of the largest African colony, Nigeria, in October 1960. In the next six years they were joined by Sierra Leone, Cyprus, Tanganyika (which later combined with independent Zanzibar as Tanzania), Jamaica, Trinidad, Uganda, Kenya, Malawi (the former Nyasaland), Malta, Zambia (the former Northern Rhodesia), Gambia, Singapore, Guyana (formerly British Guiana), Botswana (Bechuanaland), Lesotho (Basutoland), and Barbados. As soon as a dependency entered upon its independent nationhood, oversight of its relations with Britain were transferred to C.R.O. from the Colonial Office. Indeed the departmental transfer was a not unimportant symbol of the new status. As the process speeded up it became increasingly clear that the days of the Colonial Office as a separate department were numbered. And it was almost equally obvious that the residuary legatee would be the C.R.O., which had originally sprung from the loins of the Colonial Office in its heyday.

It was some time, however, before the British Government or a wide range of informed opinion was prepared to accept this conclusion. In a Commons debate on the subject in April 1954 (525 H.C.Deb., cols. 2403-99) all but one of the speakers, while not necessarily uncritical of the allocation of departmental responsibilities, were against a Colonial Office-C.R.O. merger – the one exception (Thomas Reid) being a former Colonial Service official. The Government spokesman (Henry Hopkinson, Minister of State for Colonial Affairs) claimed that the independent Commonwealth countries 'would be very unlikely to relish the idea of surrendering the right to deal with one department which represents them alone, in favour of dealing with a department which is also responsible for colonial affairs'. He was prepared to concede, however, that 'when many more of our territories . . . have passed on to full self-governing status, perhaps some redistribution of duties between the Colonial Office and the Commonwealth Relations Office will be called for'.

The movement of opinion on the subject can be gauged from the successive writings of a senior Colonial Office official, Sir Charles Jeffries, who retired as Joint Deputy Under-Secretary of State in 1956. In a book published in the same year (*The Colonial Office*, 200) he expressed the view that even if some of the territories for which the Colonial Office was responsible became independent 'in the fairly near future' the Office would still have 'immense responsibilities for as long as any planner can usefully look ahead' and Sir Charles did not see 'any prospect of reverting to the pre-1925 arrangement under which a single Secretary of State and body of officials had to deal with the affairs of the whole Commonwealth (excepting India)'. Four years later (*Transfer of Power*, 140) he was prepared to admit that a departmental merger with the C.R.O. might be 'the right thing to do', but emphasised the difficulties in the way: the volume of work for the responsible minister of the combined department and, more important, the mixing of two quite different departmental approaches. The C.R.O. approach was based on 'the principle of absolute and equal partnership, in which the United Kingdom claims no special status or authority', while the Colonial Office approach was based on the principle that, however autonomous the dependencies might in practice be, the British Government was 'finally and morally responsible for their well-being'. At best Sir Charles Jeffries thought such a mixture of approaches in the same department would be confusing, but at worst 'it might actually prejudice the proper working of one or both of the kinds of relationship'. But in an article in *The Times* of 26th July, 1963, Sir Charles felt himself able to give a cautious welcome to the proposal, since the objection to mixing the different departmental approaches no longer had the same force. From the point of view of the dependent territories the sharing of a British department with the independent Commonwealth countries 'would be a welcome enhancement of status' and would have clear practical advantages in areas in which dependencies and Commonwealth members had problems in common. It would, moreover, be in the best interests of the remaining members of the Overseas Service, whose accumulated experience might otherwise be lost.

Meanwhile the 1959–60 Select Committee on Estimates had addressed itself to an examination of the Colonial Office and had come out strongly in favour of a merger with the C.R.O. The C.R.O. itself, in its evidence to the committee, had maintained that the functions of the two departments were so fundamentally different as to militate against a merger (although it was not considered to be in the public interest to publish the evidence on which this claim was based). The C.R.O. argument for its separate existence was thus identical with that advanced fifty years before for the removal of Dominion work from the Colonial Office.

The chief C.R.O. witness before the Estimates Committee – Sir Alexander Clutterbuck, the then Permanent Under-Secretary – did not, however, completely rule out the possibility of a merger in the future. 'I personally think', he told the committee, 'that when sufficient parts of the Colonial Empire have become independent there will be so little left that it would be anomalous to have a separate department to look after it. Then I think the question [of a merger] might be approached with a better chance of success'. The difficulty that independent Commonwealth countries would feel about having their affairs 'handled by the same department as handles also the affairs of the dependent territories . . . might disappear if the great part of the Colonial territories were independent like them, with only a small residue left'. This was a criterion which clearly posed the question of when the fast-diminishing 'residue' had in fact achieved the requisite degree of smallness to warrant a departmental merger.

The chief Colonial Office witness, Sir Hilton Poynton, the Permanent Under-Secretary, was much friendlier to the idea of a merger – perhaps understandably as the representative of the contracting, rather than the expanding, department. He acknowledged, however, that in a sense 'the things that make this idea advantageous from the point of view of the newly emerging countries and the Colonial Office [e.g., increased status by association with independent countries] are precisely the reverse of the coin which makes them unattractive from the point of view of the already independent countries and the C.R.O.' Sir Hilton envisaged the new department organised in three blocks: one to deal with 'relations' – primarily with the independent Commonwealth countries – on the lines of the present C.R.O.; one to deal with administrative 'responsibilities' in the colonial field; and the third 'organised functionally with no distinction between the independent and dependent, particularly in the field of technical aid, social services, advice, and that kind of thing'. The Estimates Committee expressed its approval of this scheme and concluded, after weighing the evidence, that 'the continued existence of two separate Departments of State to deal with the affairs of a rapidly changing Commonwealth leads to a dichotomy of thought and approach that militates against the unity of the Commonwealth'.

But the Government was not yet convinced, and when the Estimates Committee's report came to be debated in the Commons in December 1960 (632 H.C.Deb., cols. 963–1024) the Colonial Secretary stated the Government's view that the time had not yet come for a merger of the Colonial Office and C.R.O. Departmental responsibilities did not remain static, however. The Colonial Secretary's statement of December 1960 had envisaged the establishment of a new department to handle technical assistance for overseas under the joint policy direction of the Foreign, Commonwealth Relations, and Colonial Offices, and in July 1961 the Department of Technical Co-operation came into being on this basis, taking staff largely from the technical assistance side of the Colonial Office (and thus contributing to the decline of that Office). South African withdrawal from the Commonwealth made it possible, in December 1961, to transfer responsibility for the High Commission Territories from the C.R.O. to the Colonial Office. And in March 1962 both Offices lost functions relating to Central Africa to yet another body with overlapping responsibilities in the field of Commonwealth affairs – the Central African Office.

In answer to questions following his announcement of the setting up of the Central African Office (655 H.C.Deb., cols. 1545–53), the Prime Minister (Macmillan) was prepared to admit that 'the day will come when the two departments [Colonial Office and C.R.O.] will be amalgamated', although 'at the present state of development of the Commonwealth' the step would be 'misunderstood' by the independent Commonwealth countries. He claimed that the removal of 'appropriate parts of the Commonwealth Relations Office and of the Colonial Office and other departments to perform a functional task' in the Department of Technical Co-operation represented a stage 'on the way to what will ultimately come – a single department – as the dependent territories become very small and almost of minor importance'. In this context, the assignment of the two Offices to a single minister, in July 1962, was clearly significant, although each department continued to retain its separate identity. A further stage came with the formation of the Douglas-Home administration in October 1963, when *all* the other ministers in the C.R.O. and the Colonial Office (two Ministers of State and three Parliamentary Under-Secretaries) were assigned to both departments. At the same time it was announced that the Central African Office would be wound up and its responsibilities re-assumed by the C.R.O. and Colonial Office.

Then, in February 1964, Sir Alec Douglas-Home announced that on 1st July, 1965, or as soon as possible after that date the much-discussed merger would in fact take place. But before this could be implemented the Conservative Government left office and its Labour successor, for reasons that were never publicly announced, delayed progress on the merger. The Wilson Government of October 1964 again included separate Secretaries of State for the Colonies and for Commonwealth Relations and only one of the other ministers in the departments (a peer) was appointed to both. This apparent indecision did not, however, prevent the Labour Party from including the amalgamation in its manifesto for the election of March 1966 as evidence of its intention to 'modernise' Whitehall. Soon after the election the Prime Minister announced that the two Offices would be combined by 1st August, 1966, and on that date the Colonial Office disappeared as a separate departmental entity. It became the Dependent Territories Division of the Commonwealth Office, as the C.R.O. was now to be called. The office of Colonial Secretary was retained for a few months longer and thus the Commonwealth Office began its new existence with two Cabinet ministers at its head.

Another change affecting departmental organisation for Commonwealth relations introduced by the Labour Government from October 1964 was the upgrading of the Department of Technical Co-operation to be the Ministry of Overseas Development. Unlike its predecessor, the Ministry of Overseas Development has responsibilities in the field of capital aid as well as technical assistance. Since over eighty-five per cent of British bilateral aid goes to Commonwealth countries (including some twenty-five per cent to India and Pakistan), the Ministry's links with the C.R.O. and the Colonial Office – and now the Commonwealth Office – were necessarily very close. The creation of a department working comprehensively in the field of development removed the one obvious disadvantage of the transfer of a colony's affairs from the Colonial Office to the C.R.O. – that the continuation of aid given to an under-developed colony did not seem appropriate when that colony had attained independence as a member of the Commonwealth.

ii. Developing Links with the Foreign Office

Although the change of title to 'Commonwealth Office' was probably inevitable with the absorption of the Colonial Office, the designation 'Commonwealth Relations Office' gave a clearer idea of what is still the major function of the combined Office – the supervision of Britain's 'Commonwealth relations'. It is thus a *diplomatic* function and has been so at least since the 1920s when the Dominions achieved equality of status with Britain and began to develop their individual international identities. Walter Runciman went to the heart of the matter when in 1925 he described the new Dominions Office as 'a Foreign Office with a friendly feeling'. In administrative terms it means that for purposes of external relations Britain makes a distinction between those countries which are members of the Commonwealth (together with the Irish Republic – a precedent which was not followed when South Africa left the Commonwealth) and those which are not. Such a division clearly raises difficulties in the implementation of an articulated external relations policy, but this may be said to be counterbalanced by the special significance of the Commonwealth relationship. Increasingly, however, doubts are expressed as to the value of the Commonwealth association to Britain, especially as the expansion of its membership brings ever greater diversity of aims and outlook. Britain alone among Commonwealth countries maintains a separate department for Commonwealth relations: elsewhere administrative recognition of the fact of the Commonwealth goes no further than a special section within a general external affairs ministry. It has long seemed that if the C.R.O. and its Dominions Office predecessor had not existed, it would have been impossible – at any rate since the end of the Second World War – to invent a Whitehall department simply for the purpose of handling Commonwealth relations. Britain as the founding and most powerful nation in the Commonwealth clearly has special reasons for emphasising the Commonwealth relationship, but has the time now come when this should no longer take the form of a separate department?

The arguments for this course are of a different kind from those which were advanced in favour of a Colonial Office-C.R.O. merger. Then there was the real problem of what to do about a fast-contracting department, rapidly losing territorial responsibilities as independent nationhood extended in the Commonwealth. A Colonial Office-C.R.O. merger seemed the easiest solution, though not without some difficulties. But the newly-enlarged Commonwealth Office is clearly a viable department and, unlike an earlier stage in the evolution of departmental organisation for Commonwealth relations, there is no discernible current demand for change from the overseas Commonwealth countries. The case for a merger with the Foreign Office can only really be argued on the grounds that (a) the departmental dichotomy leads to undesirable conflicts of policy, or (b) it would be administratively 'tidier', more logical, for external relations to be looked upon as a single major departmental function.

It was during the crises which preceded the Second World War and the war itself that a serious demand arose for the transfer of the Dominion Office's responsibilities to the Foreign Office, and the motivation was primarily the interests of the Dominions themselves. The distinguished Canadian High Commissioner in London during the period, Vincent Massey, had felt as long ago as the establishment of the Dominions Office in 1925, he records in his memoirs, that the 'one essential step towards better understanding is to bring the Dominion representatives into direct contact with the Foreign Office itself. An intermediate department, however able its staff or well-intentioned its head, will serve only to cause circumlocution, delays and misunderstandings'. A decade later, as High Commissioner, he discovered that the Dominions Office machinery delayed the transmission of information about foreign crises and wondered whether the functions of the Office could not be better performed by a Dominions section within the Foreign Office. During the war, although the flow of information was generally liberal, the Dominions frequently felt that they did not exert sufficient influence in the making of policy because it was exercised, so to speak, at second or third hand. This led to the demand that either the Dominions Secretary should be a full member of the War Cabinet or that the Dominion governments should deal directly with the Foreign Office. And it was not only the Dominions which advocated this course. In 1944 Sir William Clark, with long experience as a British high commissioner (he was the first to be appointed – to Canada – in 1928) argued that Britain and the Dominions 'would be on a more comfortable parity if our Foreign Office and Dominions Office were merged into a Department of External Affairs' (Mansergh, 1958, 403). On balance, however, Professor Mansergh has argued that it was much to the advantage of the Dominions at this period that they had a minister constantly concerned with their interests rather than an already-overburdened Foreign Secretary.

After the war the proposal continued, on occasion, to be made. In the 1954 debate on departmental responsibilities the Minister of State for Colonial Affairs rejected it out of hand since it was essential that 'there should be a special department with which Commonwealth members can deal. Our relations with each other are quite different from our relations with foreign countries'. This, however, was at a time when membership of the Commonwealth numbered eight and no indigenous African colony had yet obtained membership. As Commonwealth membership spread over a large area of the globe – including Africa and the Caribbean as well as Asia, Australasia, Europe and North America – the existence of two major departments dealing with external relations came to appear, as one observer put it, 'at best clumsy, at worst harmful' (*The Future of the Commonwealth*, 39). At least two international issues – Cyprus, and the Indonesian-Malaysia confrontation – in which both departments were concerned sometimes seemed to lead to confused, even conflicting, policies.

It was the report of the Plowden Committee on Britain's overseas representational services in February 1964 (Cmnd. 2276) which stimulated the most comprehensive and intense discussion of the question of a C.R.O.-Foreign Office merger. The Plowden Committe had been set up in 1962 partly because of the difficulty now felt in distinguishing between the nature of the work of the Foreign Office on the one hand and the C.R.O. on the other. But the more general reason for its enquiry was to see whether the organisation of the overseas services – the Foreign Service, the Commonwealth Relations Service, and the Trade Commission Service of the Board of Trade – was still appropriate in the situation which had developed since they had assumed their present form in 1943 (when the Foreign Service had been reorganised). Since then, among other things, the number of sovereign states had multiplied and international organisations were playing an increasing role in the external relations of individual countries (Beloff, 416).

The main conclusion of the Committee was that 'the division of the world, for representational purposes, into Commonwealth and non-Commonwealth countries impedes the development and execution of a coherent foreign policy'; and its principal recommendation, that the Foreign Office and C.R.O. should draw their staff from a single, unified Diplomatic Service. The committee admitted that the 'logic of events' pointed to the amalgamation of the C.R.O. and Foreign Office and recommended that this should be the ultimate aim. But it came to the conclusion that the moment was not yet opportune for a complete departmental merger. As a first step the committee believed, however, that a unified Diplomatic Service would give many of the advantages of a combined office. There would be one service engaged in what is fundamentally one job. A unified service would facilitate much greater interchange between officials with foreign and Commonwealth experience. It would also ensure that economic and commercial work in the Commonwealth (where the Trade Commission Service, unlike that in foreign countries, was separately organised at present) was brought into closer relationship with political work. It would make better use of specialist skills, especially in areas like South-East Asia and West Africa, where there is a great similarity between the problems of newly-independent countries, whether or not they happened to be members of the Commonwealth. Finally, the committee felt, a unified service would make it possible to rationalise work of the same nature: in particular, communications, training and standards of security; and it would make easier the introduction of common conditions of service. Although the two departments would retain their separate identities they would, within a unified Diplomatic Service, grow closer together in policy and practice. This was both desirable in itself and helpful if in the future a full amalgamation were carried out.

The main recommendations of the Plowden Committee were immediately accepted by the then Conservative Government, and were implemented by it or its Labour successor. Her Majesty's Diplomatic Service, initially headed by the Permanent Under-Secretary at the Foreign

Office and subsequently by the permanent head of the C.R.O., came into being on 1st January, 1965. A Diplomatic Service Administration Office was created by combining the establishments' departments of the Foreign Office and C.R.O., while joint departments were set up for information, protocol, and research. It was envisaged that the two Offices, while remaining separate, would 'draw increasingly on common services, including a joint library service, integrated research facilities, a single registry and archives system, and an integrated system of communications with all posts' (*Commonwealth Relations Office Yearbook*, 1966, 170).

There is clearly now a high degree of operational liaison between the Foreign and Commonwealth Offices. It poses the question as to whether the 'logic of events' should now be accepted and the Plowden Committee's 'ultimate aim' of a full departmental merger be implemented. The committee thought such a step would be inexpedient since it 'could be misinterpreted as implying a loss of interest in the Commonwealth'. This judgement was endorsed by the Conservative and Labour Governments – neither party wishing to appear as unfriendly to the Commonwealth idea – and by much, though by no means all, informed opinion. But, as Lord Plowden admitted in the Lords debate on his report in April 1964 (257 H.L.Deb., cols. 22–128), it is British-based, rather than overseas opinion. And it would seem at least reasonable to suppose that overseas Commonwealth members which have remained in the association despite the Suez Affair of 1956, the 1961–3 negotiations for Britain's entry into the European Economic Community, and the progressive worsening of the Rhodesian situation are not likely to blanch at the prospect of Britain's falling into line with its Commonwealth partners in having a single Ministry for External Relations.

On the British side fears have been expressed that a combined office would involve impossible burdens for its

ministerial head, and lead to a muting of the Commonwealth's voice in the Whitehall 'corridors of power'. The
first objection is, of course, impossible to evaluate. It is
significant, however, that both Lord Inchyra, a former
permanent head of the Foreign Office and a member of
the Plowden Committee, in the Lords debate on the
Plowden Report, and the Government spokesman (Nigel
Fisher) in the subsequent Commons debate in July 1964
(699 H.C.Debs., cols 1456-88) made reference to the
problems of two separate departments working in the
same field, Lord Inchyra bearing witness from his own
'rather painful experience to the confusion, delays and
. . . feeling of frustration and exasperation which is often
caused by having two Departments of State dealing with
what is really, to all intents and purposes, the same problem'. It may well be that the ministerial burden would be
lessened rather than increased if the departmental division
between relations with the Commonwealth and relations
with non-Commonwealth countries – with all the possibility of misunderstanding and unco-ordinated policies to
which it gives rise – were ended. The creation of a unified
Diplomatic Service obviously helps, but it is itself a recognition that the problem of co-ordination exists.

Would the disappearance of the Commonwealth Office
– and with it a minister who since 1945 has automatically
been a member of the Cabinet – lessen the influence of
Commonwealth factors in British policy-making? To meet
this difficulty it has been suggested (for example, by Lords
Attlee and Gladwyn in the Lords debate on the Plowden
Report) that the combined office should have two Cabinet
ministers, one of them concerned specifically with Commonwealth relations. It is not, of course, unknown for
such provision to be made: there were, for example, two
Cabinet ministers at the Air Ministry for a short period
in 1938 and at the Ministry of Power for a much longer
period between 1957 and 1959 – even before the 'double-
banking' experiments in the Macmillan Cabinet from

1962–3. Two Cabinet ministers worked side by side in the Foreign Office between 1962 and 1964, and, at least initially, in the 1966 Commonwealth Office; it could conceivably become conventional for a Prime Minister to appoint to his Cabinet a Minister for Commonwealth Relations within a combined Ministry of External Relations. But even if this should not prove possible, recent Whitehall experience with 'federalised' ministries – like the Ministry of Defence and the Department of Education and Science – may be relevant to the proposed combined ministry. University interests have not been noticeably less vocal within the Government since the Department of Education and Science took over the Treasury's function of university liaison, nor – perhaps unfortunately – have the Services ceased to press their particular points of view inside the integrated Ministry of Defence. A Ministry of External Relations, with a Commonwealth 'side' under a Minister of State, might well be perfectly adequate in giving voice to the Commonwealth viewpoint (or rather, viewpoints) in the formulation of British policy, backed, as it would be, by all those other channels, formal and informal, official and unofficial, British and overseas, for the expression of a Commonwealth consciousness.

iii. The Commonwealth Secretariat

One of the arguments used in the controversy about merging the Commonwealth and Foreign Offices concerned the role of the C.R.O. in preparing for Commonwealth Prime Ministers' Meetings – the topmost level of intergovernmental liaison – and the various other kinds of Commonwealth official conferences. Lord Alport, with experience as a C.R.O. minister and high commissioner, told the Lords during the 1964 debate on the Plowden Report that as the secretarial work for Commonwealth conferences had to be carried out in Britain it seemed logical and proper that it should be in the hands of a

G   79 special department designated for that purpose, the C.R.O. A few months later the Commonwealth Prime Ministers met and accepted the idea of a conference secretariat controlled by the Commonwealth as a whole. Thus when, in the same month (July 1964), the Commons came to debate the Plowden Report, Humphrey Berkeley (who favoured a Foreign Office-C.R.O. merger) was able to welcome this new development as more likely to give significance to the Commonwealth than the retention of the C.R.O., which was 'merely a British Government department'. The Government spokesman, Nigel Fisher, Parliamentary Under-Secretary for Commonwealth Relations and for the Colonies, denied that the creation of a Commonwealth Secretariat had any relevance to the functioning of the C.R.O., but only by minimising the Office's conference and informational work in a way which would have been virtually inconceivable by a Government spokesman before the adoption of the idea of a Commonwealth Secretariat. 'It is true', the minister said, 'that the C.R.O. has hitherto organised things like the Commonwealth Prime Minister's Conference and has always tried to help other Commonwealth members by supplying them with factual information, especially to those countries which have fewer diplomatic resources than we have. *But these are comparatively minor functions of the C.R.O.* [author's italics]. Its main responsibility has always been to ensure that Britain's policies are understood and, where possible, supported by other Commonwealth governments, that British interests in Commonwealth countries are safeguarded, and that British policy takes account of Commonwealth relations. Therefore, the functions of the Secretariat and the C.R.O. are quite different and distinct, one acting for all Commonwealth governments, the other acting for the British Government.'

The minister could prove in practice to be right but a year before the Secretariat was actually established was perhaps a little early to be categorical. Nevertheless, historically – as we have seen – there has certainly been a close relationship between the idea of a secretariat and the British department responsible for Commonwealth relations. The significance of the 1964 proposal for a secretariat was not that it was put forward – since it had many predecessors – but that it was adopted. At this stage it might be convenient to pick up the story of the secretariat at the point at which it was left in Chapter IV.

Although the Dominions played a part in the *ad hoc* secretariats for the inter-war Imperial Conferences, demands for a *permanent* Imperial Conference secretariat continued to be made (they are conveniently summarised in Harvey, *Consultation and Co-operation in the Commonwealth*). As in 1907 it was Australia, rather than the other Dominions (and particularly Canada), which was anxious to develop consultative machinery. In July 1924 the Australian Prime Minister, S. M. Bruce, proposed a secretariat which would be responsible to all the Prime Ministers and would prepare for the Imperial Conferences, service the conference when in session, follow up all its decisions, and keep the Dominions constantly informed of developments between conferences. It would be not merely a link between the individual Dominion governments and the British Government, but also one between all the Dominion governments. The proposal fell on deaf ears, however, and it was apparently never considered by the Imperial Conference as a whole. But Bruce may have got part of what he wanted when, later in the year, an Australian official (R. G. Casey) was sent as liaison officer in the British Foreign Office.

Similar proposals for a secretariat by another Australian Prime Minister, John Curtin, some twenty years later met a similar fate. Curtin's secretariat would normally have been located in London, but would function for conferences at the place of meeting, which might not necessarily be in London. It would not supersede existing direct channels of communication between governments, and its members would be responsible to their respective Prime Ministers rather than to the Imperial Conference as a whole. Curtin discussed his proposals at the 1944 Meeting of Commonwealth Prime Ministers but no mention was made in the communique issued after the meeting and certainly no action was taken.

The last of the formal Imperial Conferences had been held in 1937. The 1944 meeting was the first of the more informal – and increasingly more frequent – consultations between Commonwealth Prime Ministers (or Heads of Government) which have taken the place of the Imperial Conference in the post-war period. If the secretariat was on an *ad hoc* basis for the formally established Imperial Conference, it is perhaps not surprising that it remained so for the informal Meetings of Prime Ministers. On the British side, the Cabinet Office, in close co-operation with the C.R.O., took the lead in the process of fixing the date for each meeting and determining the subjects for discussion, and in securing departmental drafts for British ministers taking part; it also drafted the final communique for the consideration of the Prime Ministers and their advisers (Mallaby, 138–9, 148). The C.R.O. itself handled the main bulk of the actual correspondence with the other Commonwealth governments.

Until 1964 suggestions of a joint Commonwealth secretariat were resisted, on the grounds, as Duncan Sandys, then Commonwealth Secretary, put it in an official publication of January 1962 (*The Modern Commonwealth*, 11), that such an organisation 'would inevitably cut across the direct personal relations between ministers and officials in different Commonwealth countries, which is such a special feature of our association'. This may have been the specific ground for opposition but it is difficult not to believe, in view of the past history of such proposals, that a secretariat came under the heading of 'centralised machinery for the consideration of political questions, especially foreign policy and defence', to which, as every issue of the *Commonwealth Relations Office List* from 1956 to 1964 recorded, 'some of the Members have been inflexibly opposed'. Certainly, when in 1948, Lord Bruce, as he now was, revived his 1924 secretariat proposals in the course of a debate in the House of Lords (Mansergh, 1952, i, 597–604), the Commonwealth Secretary, Lord Addison, mentioned as one of the principal disadvantages of a secretariat that 'it might get into the habit of wanting to exercise authorities which the Commonwealth countries would insist upon exercising through their own governments'.

At a Meeting of Commonwealth Prime Ministers in July 1964, however, there was a dramatic change. Apparently as a result of African and West Indian pressure – with President Nkrumah of Ghana, President Kenyatta of Kenya, and Dr. Eric Williams, Prime Minister of Trinidad, as principal advocates – the meeting decided to instruct a group of officials drawn from the various governments to consider the best basis for establishing a Commonwealth Secretariat in order, as the final communique put it, that 'some permanent expression' should be given to the desire, evident in its discussions, 'for closer and more informed' understanding between Commonwealth governments. The Secretariat was to be 'available *inter alia* to disseminate factual information to member countries, to assist existing agencies, both official and unofficial, in the promotion of Commonwealth links, and to help to co-ordinate preparations for meetings of Commonwealth heads of Government and, where appropriate, for meetings of other Commonwealth Ministers'.

This was a decided reversal of existing trends and it is difficult to do more than speculate about the motivation for it. It could well have been that African members were dissatisfied with the way in which the Rhodesian problem – of immense significance to them if strictly speaking within the 'domestic jurisdiction' of the United Kingdom – had been dealt with at the conference, resulting in a desire to remove the main initiative in drawing up the 'agenda' from the British Government. Some dissatisfaction had also been expressed that not all the information sent out by the C.R.O. went to all members (it had always been officially admitted that a selection was made, so as to avoid sending members information on topics in which they were not interested). The Secretariat may also have been looked upon, in the words of *The Times* (4th January, 1965), as a body which would 'complete the "decolonising" process by taking the management of the Commonwealth itself out of British hands'.

But having taken the decision to establish the Secretariat the Commonwealth governments encountered difficulties in formulating its actual powers and in appointing its head. After some months of discussion Commonwealth officials met in London in January 1965 under the chairmanship of the British Cabinet Secretary and submitted an agreed report to all the governments. No action was taken on this – presumably because of continuing disagreements – and the officials met again immediately before the June 1965 Meeting of Commonwealth Prime Ministers. The main division, according to *The Times* (15th June, 1965), was 'between those governments who want a dynamic personality as Secretary-General to get the new organisation off to a good start, and those who fear that anyone but the most retiring official might get it off to much too good a start'. The first group thought the project might die of inanition unless some faith was shown at the preliminary stage, while the second group feared that 'anything but a post office may burgeon into a super-Commonwealth state'.

The difficulties were eventually ironed out. A distinguished Canadian diplomatist, Arnold Smith, was appointed Secretary-General (he took up his duties at Marlborough House, London, in August 1965) and the Commonwealth Prime Ministers published with their final communique on 26th June an agreed memorandum on the powers of the Secretariat (*Commonwealth Relations Office Yearbook*, 1966, 25–31).

The memorandum, true to the leading theme of Commonwealth development, emphasises that the Commonwealth does not encroach on the sovereignty of individual members, nor require its members to seek to reach collective decisions or take united action. The Secretariat must thus be seen to be the servant of the Commonwealth countries collectively and not arrogate to itself any executive functions. Nevertheless the memorandum sets out a number of constructive tasks for the Secretariat to tackle. It will serve the Commonwealth governments by facilitating and promoting consultation on matters of common concern. This will include the dissemination of information on, among other things, the constitutional advance of the remaining dependent territories, economic problems and social and cultural issues. In so doing it will gradually accumulate 'a body of knowledge and experience which will contribute to an even closer understanding among member-governments'. The Secretariat may also play a role in assisting member-governments, at their request, in obtaining development aid and technical assistance on a multilateral or bilateral Commonwealth basis. Another major task will be to review existing organisations within the Commonwealth concerned with economic and related affairs with a view to avoiding unnecessary duplication, deciding which activities might usefully be absorbed by the Secretariat, and fostering co-operation between the Secretariat and other Commonwealth bodies. The cost of the Secretariat is to be borne by all member countries, with Britain, Canada, India and Australia between them accounting for over two-thirds.

It is too early to assess the value of the Secretariat. Its powers are carefully restricted but capable of development. Certainly there seems to be no danger of it encroaching on individual members' autonomy. The Rhodesian independence crisis came to a climax only a few months after the Secretariat was established and although it was responsible for servicing the Commonwealth Prime Ministers' Meeting on the question in Lagos in January 1966, and the subsequent meeting in London in September, there was no evidence that the existence of a secretariat affected the train of events in any material way: indeed, some members were disappointed that it had not been able to ensure that the second Rhodesian meeting was held six months after the first (that is, in July), as the Lagos meeting had provided, rather than allow it to be delayed until September – presumably at Britain's request. Whether the Secretariat, as it develops, will serve to infuse new significance into the Commonwealth association, which for so long has depended ultimately upon Britain's membership and constructive interest, still remains to be seen.

The question most relevant to the present study is the implication of the establishment of a Commonwealth Secretariat for the Whitehall department specifically concerned with Britain's Commonwealth relationships. It is unlikely that the proposal was viewed in the C.R.O. as unfavourably as similar projects sixty years ago were received by its departmental predecessor. No longer does Britain have any direct responsibility for, or control over, the defence and foreign policy of other Commonwealth member countries (except where there are explicit treaty obligations), and thus a secretariat can operate in this field – if members will let it – without affecting the functions of the Commonwealth Office. Clearly the Office will lose a good deal of its responsibilities for Commonwealth conference arrangements and general information work, although, as we have seen, men with ministerial experience in the C.R.O. (Lord Alport and Nigel Fisher) have given different accounts of how important these responsibilities were. On the other hand, there will be the additional responsibility of liaison with the Secretariat itself. The establishment of the Secretariat certainly does not weaken the argument for a Foreign Office-Commonwealth Office merger, and many will feel that in fact it substantially strengthens it (Beloff, 415; Robinson, 1964, 421).

This study of the development of British departmental organisation for Commonwealth relations has been primarily historical in treatment. It ends in 1966 when, once again, there is a single department to deal with both dependent and self-governing Commonwealth countries but when, at the same time, there is considerable speculation about the future of the newly-combined Commonwealth Office. It does not require much gift of prophecy to foresee the time when the whole process of providing a separate Whitehall centre for the Commonwealth relationship has itself become a matter of history.

Bibliography

GENERAL WORKS

On the general topic to which this study relates – the development and structure of the Commonwealth – the following are particularly valuable.

MILLER, J. D. B., (1965), *The Commonwealth in the World*, 3rd edn., Duckworth.

WALKER, P. GORDON, (1962), *The Commonwealth*, Secker and Warburg.

WHEARE, K. C., (1961), *The Constitutional Structure of the Commonwealth*, Oxford U.P.

WISEMAN, H. VICTOR, (1965), *Britain and the Commonwealth*, Allen and Unwin.

SOURCES

A. *Unpublished*

Colonial Office Records in the Public Record Office (Unpublished Crown-copyright material has been reproduced by permission of the Controller of H.M. Stationery Office)

C.O. 209/274, No. 8300 of March 1911 (Office minutes on direct communication)

C.O. 323/503, No. 11053 of April 1905 (Office minutes on Imperial Council)

C.O. 323/511, No. 10975 of April 1905 (Graham's

memorandum of December 1904; Office minutes on the Lyttelton dispatch)

C.O. 323/534, No. 29255A of August 1907 (C.O. letter to Treasury)

C.O. 532/7, No. 38604 of October 1908 (Hopwood's minute on the role of the Secretariat)

C.O. 532/16, No. 35842 of October 1909 (Lucas's observations on his Australasian tour)

C.O. 532/35, No. 25309 of August 1911 (Just's memorandum of December 1910; memoranda on direct communication; Seely's and Harcourt's Cabinet papers)

C.O. 537/1035 (E. J. Harding's memorandum on direct communication of May 1922)

C.O. 886/4, Nos. 25 and 29 (Just's memorandum and Lucas's Cabinet paper of July 1910).

(Herbert, Viscount) *Gladstone Papers*, British Museum Additional Manuscripts 45985–46118.

London University Ph.D. Theses

CROSS, J. A., 'The Dominions Department of the Colonial Office: Origins and Early Years, 1905–1914', 1965.

KENDLE, J. E., 'The Colonial and Imperial Conferences, 1887–1911: A Study in Imperial Organisation and Politics', 1965. (Quoted by permission of the author).

B. Published

AMERY, L. S., (1953), *My Political Life*, 3 vols., Hutchinson.

AMERY, L. S., (1912), *Union and Strength*, Arnold.

BELOFF, MAX, 'The Foreign and Commonwealth Services' in *Public Administration*, 42, (1964), 415-9.

BORDEN, H. (ed.), (1938), *Robert Laird Borden: His Memoirs*, 2 vols., Macmillan.

Cambridge History of the British Empire, vol. III (1959), *The Empire-Commonwealth, 1870-1919*, Cambridge U.P.

Command Papers (H.M.S.O.)

Cd. 5545 (1888), Report of the Ridley Commission on the Civil Service.

Cd. 2785 (1905), Lyttelton's dispatch.

Cd. 3523 (1907), Proceedings of the Colonial Conference of 1907.

Cd. 3795 (1907), Elgin's dispatch on Colonial Office re-organisation.

Cd. 5745 (1911), Proceedings of the Imperial Conference of 1911.

Cmnd. 2276 (1964), Plowden Report on Representational Services Overseas.

Commonwealth Relations Office List, H.M.S.O., annually 1951-65.

Commonwealth Relations Office Yearbook, H.M.S.O., 1966.

CROSS, J. A., 'The Colonial Office and the Dominions before 1914, in *Journal of Commonwealth Political Studies*, IV (1966), 138-148.

CROSS, J. A., 'Whitehall and the Commonwealth' in *Journal of Commonwealth Political Studies*, II (1964), 189-206. (Material from this, and the preceding, article reproduced by permission of the Editors and the Publishers, Leicester University Press.)

Dominions Office and Colonial Office List, H.M.S.O., annually, 1926-40.

EAYRS, JAMES, (1961), *The Art of the Possible: Government and Foreign Policy in Canada*, University of Toronto Press.

Estimates, Select Committee on, Third Report from, Session 1958-59, *The Commonwealth Relations Office*, H.M.S.O., H.C.252,1959.

Estimates, Select Committee on, Fourth Report from, Session 1959-60, *The Colonial Office*, H.M.S.O., H.C.260, 1960.

FARR, D. M. L., (1955), *The Colonial Office and Canada, 1867-1887*, Oxford U.P.

FIDDES, SIR GEORGE, (1926), *The Dominions and Colonial Offices*, Putnam.

The Future of the Commonwealth: A British View, H.M.S.O. 1963.

HALL, H. DUNCAN, (1920), *The British Commonwealth of Nations*, Methuen.

HALL, H. DUNCAN, 'The Genesis of the Balfour Declaration of 1926', in *Journal of Commonwealth Political Studies*, I (1961-3), 169-193.

HARVEY, HEATHER J., (1952), *Consultation and Co-operation in the Commonwealth*, Oxford U.P.

JEFFRIES, SIR CHARLES, (1956), *The Colonial Office*, Allen and Unwin.

JEFFRIES, SIR CHARLES, (1960), *Transfer of Power*, Pall Mall Press.

JOHNSON, F. A., (1960), Defence by Committee: *The British Committee of Imperial Defence*, Oxford U.P.

KEITH, A. B., (1928), *Responsible Government in the Dominions*, 2 vols., 2nd edn., Oxford U.P.

KENDLE, J. E., 'The Round Table Movement, New Zealand and the Imperial Conference of 1911' in *Journal of Commonwealth Political Studies*, III (1965), 104-17.

LA NAUZE, J. A., (1966), *Alfred Deakin*, 2 vols., Melbourne U.P./Cambridge U.P.

LONG, LORD, (1923), *Memories*, Hutchinson.

MACKENZIE, W. J. M., and GROVE, J. W., (1957), *Central Administration in Britain*, Longmans.

MACKINTOSH, JOHN P., (1962), *The British Cabinet*, Stevens.

MALLABY, SIR GEORGE, (1965), *From My Level*, Hutchinson.

MANSERGH, NICHOLAS, (1952), *Documents and Speeches on British Commonwealth Affairs, 1931-1952*, 2 vols., Oxford U.P.

MANSERGH, NICHOLAS, (1963), *Documents and Speeches on British Commonwealth Affairs, 1952-1962*, Oxford U.P.

MANSERGH, NICHOLAS, (1952), *Survey of British Commonwealth Affairs: Patterns of External Policy, 1931-1939*, Oxford U.P.

MANSERGH, NICHOLAS, (1958), *Survey of British Commonwealth Affairs: Problems of Wartime Co-operation and Post-War Change, 1939-1952*, Oxford U.P.

MASSEY, VINCENT, (1963), *What's Past is Prologue*, Macmillan.

MILLER, J. D. B., 'The C.R.O. and Commonwealth Relations' in *International Studies*, New Delhi, II (1960-1), 42-59.

NEATBY, H. BLAIR, (1963), *William Lyon Mackenzie King, Vol. II, 1924-32: The Lonely Heights*, University of Toronto Press/Methuen.

PALMER, G. E. H., (1934), *Consultation and Co-operation in the British Commonwealth*, Oxford U.P.

PARKINSON, SIR COSMO, (1947), *The Colonial Office From Within, 1909-45*, Faber.

Parliamentary Debates

    Commons   18 H.C.Deb., cols. 956-1070 (29.6.1910).

                184 H.C.Deb., cols. 2239-40 (11.6.1925).

                187 H.C.Deb., cols. 66-8 (27.7.1925).

                525 H.C.Deb., cols. 2403-99 (2.4.1954).

                632 H.C.Deb., cols. 963-1024 (19.12.1960).

                655 H.C.Deb., cols. 1545-53 (15.3.1962).

                699 H.C.Deb., cols. 1456-88 (29.7.1964).

    Lords   257 H.L.Deb., cols. 22-128 (7.4.1964).

PUGH, R. B., 'The Colonial Office, 1801-1925' in *Cambridge History of the British Empire*, Vol. III, Cambridge U.P., (1959), 711-68.

PUGH, R. B., (1964), *The Records of the Colonial and Dominions Offices*, H.M.S.O.

ROBINSON, KENNETH, 'The Intergovernmental Machinery of Commonwealth Co-operation and Consultation' in *A Decade of the Commonwealth, 1955-1964* (ed. W. B. Hamilton, Kenneth Robinson and C. D. W. Goodwin), Duke University Press, Durham, North Carolina, (1966), 89-123.

ROBINSON, KENNETH, 'A Single Ministry?' in *Public Administration*, 42, (1964), 420-2.

SANDYS, DUNCAN, (1962), *The Modern Commonwealth*, H.M.S.O.

SINCLAIR, KEITH, (1955), *Imperial Federation*, Institute of Commonwealth Studies.

SKELTON, O. D., (1922), *Life and Letters of Sir Wilfred Laurier*, 2 vols., Oxford U.P.

TYLER, J. E., 'Development of the Imperial Conference, 1887-1914' in *Cambridge History of the British Empire*, Vol. III, Cambridge U.P., (1959), 406-37.